When Chores Were Done

~boyhood stories~

by Jerry Apps

Amherst Press
Minocqua, Wisconsin

Copyright © 1999 Jerold W. Apps, author
Steve Apps, photographer

First edition
Second printing

The Guest Cottage, Inc.
dba Amherst Press
9587 Country Club Road
PO Box 1341
Minocqua, WI 54548

Cover photograph, Jerry Apps, 1937.

Library of Congress Cataloging-in-Publication Data

Apps, Jerold W. 1934-
    When Chores Were Done / by Jerry Apps; photos by Steve Apps.
        p. cm.
    ISBN 0-942495-84-5
    1. Chain 0' Lakes Region (Wis.)~Social life and customs.
2. Apps, Jerold W., 1934 —Childhood and youth. 3. Farm life—
Wisconsin—Chain 0' Lakes Region. 4. Chain 0' Lakes Region
(Wis.)—Biography. I. Title.
F587.W3A56 1999
977.598—dc21   98-48776

Printed in Canada

Dedication

To my brothers, Donald and Darrel;
to neighbor boys, David and Jim Kolka;
and to all those who lived in the
Chain O' Lake community during my growing-up years.

Contents

Acknowledgments

Several people helped with this book. My twin brothers, Donald and Darrel, deserve special mention. They read much of the manuscript, especially the stories in which they were involved. As usual with this type of material, there are differences of opinion about what happened and when. Anyone wanting a slightly different version of some of these stories should contact my brothers.

Jim Kolka, a friend from my childhood years, and his sister, Evelyn, read "Frank, Pinky, and Harry" and shared valuable background information about their father.

A special thank you to Joe and Dora Vanderstappen of rural Brussels, Wisconsin, and Laverne and Betty Forest, who own and operate Eplegaarden Orchard in rural Fitchburg, Wisconsin. Several of the book's photographs were taken at these two locations.

My son, Steve, staff photographer for the *Wisconsin State Journal*, took the photos for this book and read many drafts of the material. In addition to his skills as a photographer, he is a hard-nosed journalist. I scrapped several draft stories at his suggestion, and I changed many more following his comments. Susan Horman, an elementary teacher trained in reading and my daughter, read much of the manuscript. In her quiet way, she had considerable influence on the manuscript. My youngest son, Jeff, a Colorado businessman, also read several stories and offered useful comments.

My wife, Ruth, read every word of this book several times. Having grown up on a farm herself, she keeps me honest and on track with my writing.

Liz McBride, my tireless editor who has so far edited four of my books, has had and continues to have a profound influence on my work. She knows how to ask the right question, and how to push me toward writing beyond what I thought I could do.

And she does it with grace and humor.

Finally, my continuing thanks to all the folks at Amherst Press who work in the background to publish and promote my books. Special thanks to Chuck and Roberta Spanbauer, who have believed in my work from the beginning and continue to do so.

Echoes from the Land

It is mid-August, and I'm standing at the edge of a large field on my farm. A slight breeze blows from the southwest. The field where I stand is no longer cultivated; hasn't been for more than forty years. Yet among the wild grasses that have returned to this land that was once prairie—big bluestem, little bluestem, Indian grass—the remnants of corn rows are still evident.

I look across the field of waving plants, and I listen to the wind. The wind has always been a great mystery to me, one of nature's powerful, invisible forces. Beyond the wind, I hear sounds from an earlier time, reminders of my growing-up years on a farm located less than two miles from where I'm standing. I hear whispers from the past—quiet sounds that are easily overrun by the hurry-up noise of today. I strain my ears for these sounds, which are filled with mystery and meaning. They are like echoes that bounce from hillside to hillside, roll down the valleys, and tumble across the pond.

The sounds I hear are those of farm life before electricity, before giant tractors and self-propelled combines, before school buses hauled country children to village schools, before family farms became economic challenges that force many farmers from the land.

I hear the sounds of oat plants waving in the wind, the yellow heads ripening in the August sun, waiting for the grain binder pulled by a team of horses to clatter around the field, severing the grain stems and tying them into bundles.

I hear the threshing machine and the hearty, often bragging talk of the workers as they pitch oat bundles into the maw of the huge, vibrating thresher that separates grain from straw.

I hear a howling, menacing May wind that begins in the early morning, continues throughout the day and into the night, increasing in intensity with each passing hour. I hear tree limbs snapping and windows rattling throughout the long, frightening night. I hear Pa shouting at daybreak that the barn is toppling and the animals are trapped. I hear the screams of calves, cows, and horses, and the bellowing of the herd bull, a cry of fear rather than rage.

I hear the school bell announcing the beginning of the fall term at Chain O' Lake School. The sound of the cast-iron bell carries through the valley and slides over the hills, telling all of school days.

Away in the distance I hear our farm dog, Fanny, barking as she rounds up our small herd of Holstein cattle and shepherds them along the cow path that twists its way up the lane back of the barn to the pasture beyond the strawberry patch. Fanny has been gone for many years, yet the sound of her bark is as real as if she were fetching the cows today, saving me hiking to the back pasture.

I hear my brothers, mother, and father sitting around the kitchen table eating supper, talking about the weather, about what has to be done, about a chance to go fishing on Saturday if we get the job done by then.

I hear the sounds of the first thaw in spring, when water begins dripping from the barn roof and snow makes a mushy sound when I walk in it. I hear the call of Canada geese winging north, their V's sometimes stretching from horizon to horizon.

There is the music of meadowlarks and red-winged blackbirds, mourning doves, and house wrens, and the squeak of harness leather while Pa cuts hay with the McCormick mower.

In summer there are the sounds of city relatives: "Could you fetch another pail of water?" "Why do you get up so early?" The sounds of firecrackers and boat oars squeaking, the hay-fork rope groaning as hay is pulled from the hay wagon into the barn.

In fall the sounds become those of harvest, dry corn leaves rattling in the wind, fresh-dug potatoes tumbling down the chute to the cellar, cattle in the barn shaking their stanchions and rustling the hay pile in front of them.

In winter comes the quiet of first snow turning a drab gray-brown countryside into an expanse of white. Children at the country school laugh as they slide downhill, play fox and geese, and lob snowballs at each other. There are the sounds of the school Christmas programs where every pupil has a part from the smallest first-grader to the older, more knowing eighth-graders.

These and more are the sounds of farm life that I hear as I stand on the hill back of my farm. These sounds come from my memories of country life during the late 1930s through the 1950s. They remind me of stories from the land, stories that express deeper meanings from the perspective of one who lived them.

Winter Delivery

I knew something wasn't right with Ma, but I couldn't figure out what it was. She seemed a little plumper, but most of the neighbor women were on the plump order so that didn't seem important. She was a lot more tired than usual; often I found her sitting on a chair in the kitchen, trying to catch her breath. I hoped she wasn't sick.

"Ma sick?" I asked Pa one day when we were carrying in wood from the woodshed.

"No, she's not sick. She's expecting."

"Expecting what?" I asked.

"A new brother or sister for you," Pa said.

I thought about that a little, but didn't say anything. I was quite happy just the way things were. What would we do with a new baby in the house? Ma seemed busy enough taking care of Pa and me, cooking, washing clothes, feeding the chickens, gathering eggs, and doing all the things farm women did.

"You're gonna have to help out more around the house until the baby comes, and after, too," Pa said. "Ma needs all the help she can get."

I wasn't yet four years old, but Pa figured I was big enough to help dry dishes, carry in wood, and do other chores around the house.

We were in the midst of a long, hard winter. Snow had begun falling in November and had continued every week or so right past Christmas and into the new year of 1938. Several times wind-driven snow closed the road trailing past our farm and we were snowbound. Ma had long before grown accustomed to such weather and had an ample supply of sugar and flour so we could go a week or more and not be inconvenienced in the least for food. Of course we had our own eggs, milk, butter, smoked ham and bacon,

shelves of canned vegetables and fruits, a huge pile of potatoes, plenty of rutabagas, dill and sweet pickles, and an ever-present crock of sauerkraut that Ma dug into nearly every day. She baked, fried, and boiled sauerkraut either by itself or with pork hocks, pork chops, or ham.

Drifted roads were far less a problem for us getting out than for the milkman getting in to pick up our milk each day. The cows continued giving milk, no matter what the weather; they seemed not at all concerned about road conditions and the intensity of the winter. Pa had enough extra ten-gallon milk cans for about three days of milk. By using all the pans, kettles, and tubs around the house we could store the milk for one more day. After that, conditions became serious. We could dump the milk, but dumping milk was like tossing dollar bills into a fire. We depended on the milk for our income.

When the roads were closed for more than four days—it happened once or twice a winter—Ma made cottage cheese from some of the milk, and butter from the cream. The pigs and calves drank milk until their bellies stuck out.

Pa drove to town in early January to have grist ground for the cows and to pick up some essentials at the mercantile store. Upon returning, he said, "Couldn't even see the fence posts along the road the snow is so deep. So windy today I could hardly see to drive with the snow sifting over the top of the snow banks."

Ma shook her head but didn't say anything. She looked concerned. I wondered if she was worrying about the new baby.

I should have asked Pa when the baby was coming. If Ma was expecting, there must be a time, but I was so taken aback by the idea of a new brother or sister that I didn't think to ask. New babies were not something I thought about. I was more concerned with my sled and playing with the toy farm I'd gotten for Christmas. I'd heard Pa talk about when a cow was due, and I knew that meant she was going to have a calf; same thing for sow pigs. I was wondering if any of those facts about farm animals applied to people, especially your own mother.

On the thirtieth of January it started snowing again. The storm began as a few scattered flakes that flew on the wind and seemed to disappear into nowhere, but soon the snow began accumulating. Pa came in from the morning chores, shook the snow off his barn cap, hung up his coat, and held his hands over the woodstove to warm them.

"Looks like a bad one, Eleanor," he said as he rubbed his hands together. "Wind's pickin' up and the snow keeps comin' down harder."

I looked out the kitchen window toward the barn and could see nothing but white. It was as if someone had pulled a bedsheet down in front of the window. I couldn't even make out the outline of the barn.

Throughout the morning the snow continued, small, sharp flakes that began accumulating on the kitchen porch as the wind whistled around the corner of the woodshed and rattled the dining-room windows.

Fanny, our farm dog, ordinarily spent winter nights in the kitchen, sleeping by the cookstove. During the day she was outside, romping in the woods, bounding through the snow. Not today. She looked out the kitchen window and decided that resting by the stove was a good way to wait out the storm.

Ma cooked up a big pot of vegetable soup for dinner. The soup, along with fresh bread Ma had baked in the morning, was just right for a snowy day.

But Ma didn't eat anything. "I don't feel very good," she said. "Think I'll rest on the couch in the dining room."

During the winter months, we closed off most of the house, except for the kitchen, dining room, and Ma and Pa's bedroom. In the summer I slept upstairs, but in winter my bedroom was a closet off Ma and Pa's room.

While the storm continued raging, Ma rested on the dining-room couch. Pa went out to the woodshed occasionally and kept the cookstove and dining-room heater well stocked with wood. Even though the windows rattled while the wind tore around the corners of the house, it was warm inside. Pleasantly warm and peaceful, except I began to worry about Ma. She wasn't one to spend the afternoon on the couch.

She and Pa had some whispered conversations during the afternoon. I wondered what secrets they were keeping from me. This was something they usually did around Christmas time. But Christmas was more than a month past. I expected they were talking about the weather, but then why were they whispering? We'd been talking about the weather all winter and nobody had whispered about it.

When Pa came into the house after the evening milking, he fixed supper for the two of us. Ma said she didn't want anything to eat and we should help ourselves. Now I knew something was wrong, very wrong. Ma never, ever missed fixing meals for us.

"What's wrong with Ma?" I asked.

"Not feeling very good. Has to do with the baby," Pa said.

I knew the baby was going to be a problem for the family. It wasn't even here yet and already it was causing problems. Pa was the most awful cook who ever tried to heat beans on a woodstove. In fact, it was Ma who once said that she thought Pa couldn't heat water without burning it. He had smiled when she said that. He never claimed to know how to cook and only did it when he had to. This was one of those times. He heated up a cast-iron skillet, smeared the bottom with bacon grease, and then forked in several piles of sauerkraut fresh from the crock that we kept under the stairway in the pantry. Soon the smell of fried sauerkraut filled the kitchen, along with the smells of oak smoke and Pa's barn coat drying on its hook near the stove. Pa and I quietly ate pieces of ring bologna, homemade bread, and, of course, fried sauerkraut. The only sound was that of the wind and snow pounding against the house. It was a scary sound, especially with Ma sick.

Pa went into the dining room to check on Ma, and soon I heard him on the telephone. Pa almost never used the telephone; Ma made all the calls. I couldn't make out what Pa was saying, only now and then a word. I heard him say "schoolhouse" and "county road" and "horses". That's all I was able to make out.

"You're gonna sleep upstairs tonight, Jerold," Pa said.

This came as a surprise because during the winter I always slept downstairs.

Pa lighted the little kerosene lamp that had been my Grandmother Witt's, and he led the way up the steep stairway, along the frigid hall, to the middle room. This had a black stovepipe in it, which thrust through the floor from the dining room and entered the chimney near the ceiling. It was cool in this room, but not near as cold as the stairway and the hall.

Pa set the lamp down on the dresser, pulled the covers back on the old wooden bed, and said, "Hop in. You'll be as cozy as a bug in a rug." I didn't know much about bugs in rugs, but I did as Pa said. When I was all settled in, Pa took the lamp and made his way down the hall. I heard the door on the stairway close.

I thought some about Ma and hoped she would feel better in the morning, but mostly I listened to the wind shaking the windows in the bedroom and making scary sounds as it whistled around the corners of the house.

It seemed like I had scarcely gotten to sleep when I heard Pa saying, "Time to get up, Jerold. Time to get up."

It was light in the room, so I knew it was morning. I glanced around, at first not remembering where I was. A little pile of snow had accumulated on the sill of the room's windows, and they were so covered with frost that I couldn't see outside. The wind had stopped blowing so I figured the storm must have passed.

I gathered up my pants and shirt—I had worn my socks and long underwear to bed—and hustled down the cold hall and stairway to the dining room.

I couldn't believe my eyes when I opened the stairway door to the dining room. I was immediately drawn to the dining-room table, to which someone had added extra boards, like we did at threshing time. The table was covered with white sheets, and on the sheets were two little babies, red as beets and kicking like everything.

I must have been standing there with my mouth hanging open when Pa said, "Come over and meet your new brothers. You got twin brothers."

With my overalls and flannel shirt in hand, I gingerly walked around the dining-room table. I noticed the Round Oak heater was much hotter than usual. It was cherry-red all around the bottom. I looked these two little babies over. One was a skinny little guy, the other one a little plumper.

"What do you think?" Pa asked.

I didn't have a word to say. What words do you use when you don't think much of the idea of having a new baby in the house, and then there are two of them? The situation was beyond words. Mrs. Miller stood off to the side, a big smile on her face as she looked at me and then looked at my red-skinned twin brothers kicking away on the dining-room table.

Later, I got the story about the night's activities. The phone call Pa had made was to the doctor. Because our road was impassable, Pa said he'd meet the doctor at the school that was at the intersection of our road and the county trunk road, which the snowplows kept open. Pa had hitched the team to the bobsled, piled the sled high with blankets and robes, and set off across the fields. He picked up the doctor, and then stopped for Mrs. Miller, who often helped as a midwife. By the time I had gotten up, Pa had already taken the doctor back to his car.

A big discussion took place around what to name these two little boys. Having twins was a surprise. I suspect Ma and Pa had picked out names for a boy or a girl. Now they had to come up with names for twins. Picking out a child's name was no small task, I later learned. There were so many things to consider. You certainly didn't want to name a child after a relative with a shady reputation, or even after a horse with less than stellar credentials. Ma had named me Jerold before she realized that my Uncle Wilbur had a horse named Jerry who was right close to worthless. She never would call me Jerry for fear I would somehow be mixed up with this worthless horse.

Ma and Pa fussed over twin names for some time. If the babies had been twin girls they could have called them Betty and Bernice or Mary and Martha, perfectly good twin names. But what about twin names for boys? Finally they settled on Darrel and Donald. The job was only half finished, however. There also had to be middle names that sounded right for twins. They decided on Irvin and Arvin. Donald

Irvin and Darrel Arvin.

When the twins got a little older, and I was a lot older, it seemed clumsy to say Donald and Darrel when you meant to talk about both of them. You could say Don and Dar, but who wanted to be called Dar? So it seemed some nicknames were in order. Everyone knew about Donald Duck, so Donald became Duck. And Darrel, from the time he was old enough to eat solid food, liked potatoes, which some people called murphies. So Darrel became Murf. Duck and Murf was so much easier to say than Donald and Darrel, and those nicknames stuck with my brothers all through their growing-up years, right through high school.

As the years passed, the memory of the night my twin brothers was born has never left me. All three of us were born in the same room, but I don't recall anyone saying that I lay kicking on the dining-room table in front of a roaring woodstove. Maybe the difference was that I was born in July—a reasonable month for a birth.

Chain O' Lake School

I knew something big was in the wind shortly after my fifth birthday in July. My mother had been talking to Mrs. Hudziak who lived down on County Highway A, a couple of miles from our farm. I also noticed Ma and Pa talking a lot, but whenever I came around they shifted to a low whisper. This was not a good sign because I figured they must have been talking about me.

For a long time I wondered what was going on. Were conditions so tough in 1939 that maybe they were planning to send me off to stay with some relative? After all, I did have twin brothers and there were five mouths to feed. We all three needed new shoes about once a year, and a new pair of bib overalls, a couple of pairs of socks, some underwear, and some shirts. All of this cost money, and I knew that money was mighty short.

One day in early August Ma asked me what I thought about starting school. Now I realized what all the hushed discussions had been about. She said that Norman Hudziak, who was a year older than me, was beginning school, and Mrs. Hudziak wanted someone to join him.

"I've never been to school," I said. "But that would probably be all right."

Actually I had been to school, to the annual Christmas program. Somehow I guessed that the Christmas program wasn't very much like what happened in that schoolroom most of the school year. I soon found out that I was right about that.

I tried not to let Ma and Pa know how excited I was about going to school. But every chance I got I let my twin brothers know that I was special because I was going to school and they'd have to wait four more years before they could attend. They didn't seem the least impressed with my good fortune, but how much could kids only a year-and-half old know anyway? They couldn't even talk.

Chain O' Lake was the name of our country school, one mile south of our farm. It was also the name of our community. Every rural community was named after its local school in those days. The country schools were about four miles apart so no student had to walk much more than two miles one-way to get there.

About a half-mile south of the school, in a deep valley, lay Chain O' Lake, a single land-locked lake, unattached to any other and with no streams running in or out of it. Just over the hill from Chain O' Lake was another lake, and another after that. In one sense the lakes were a chain, but in another sense they weren't. They were like a string of pearls, except the pearls were not attached to each other. Would you call such a group of pearls a string or merely a collection? Such was the dilemma with these lakes.

Some people, especially those who lived in town and didn't know better, insisted that Chain O' Lake was really Chain O' Lakes. They argued that it made no sense to have something named Chain O' Lake because the name implied more than one lake. The logic was right, but the application was wrong. I learned then and many times since that everything that is logical is not necessarily the way it is.

The starting day for school rolled around after several slow weeks on the farm. Why is it that when you are waiting for something good to happen time drags along so slowly? Then the day arrived and I was in my little desk in the front of the schoolroom, not far from where Miss Piechowski, a black-haired, dark-eyed, rather friendly woman, sat behind her big teacher's desk.

Each desk had an inkwell. That's what Miss Piechowski said it was when I asked. She went on to explain why they were empty. She said, "The tendency for mischief, such as dipping the pigtail of the girl sitting in front of you, is usually too great for even the most well-behaved pupil." I didn't understand all the big words she used, but I caught the gist of their meaning.

The writing surface of the desk could be lifted,

and here I could store books, pencils, rulers, and other essential equipment, such as rubber bands for shooting spit wads.

Larger desks were in back of the room; smaller ones in front. Each desk was large enough for two students, but school numbers were small enough so each of us could have our own desk.

A blackboard stretched across the front of the schoolroom. Written across the top of it was the official way to make cursive letters, that's what Miss Piechowski called the writing. I soon discovered that first-graders printed. So I ignored the fancy flowing lines that were supposed to be my guide for formal handwriting.

An American flag stood on a stand near one corner of the teacher's desk, and faded pictures of George Washington and Abraham Lincoln peered down on me from their locations above the blackboard.

A set of maps, each map like a window shade, was located to the left of the blackboard. What wonderful things these maps were. On that first day of school, Miss Piechowski asked one of the older pupils to pull down the map of the United States. I had never

before seen a map of the U.S. and stared at all the wonderful colors—green for Wisconsin, yellow for Minnesota, purple for Iowa, except that day I didn't know which state was which. It quickly occurred to me that learning something about maps was something I would probably have to do before I left this place.

While I was staring at the map of the U.S., the strangest thing happened. Without any warning the map shot back up into the rack, making a terrible racket and evoking laughter from everyone but the teacher. The pupil who had pulled the map down had failed to hook the map over the little nail on the bottom of the blackboard.

In the back of the schoolroom stood a big, old wood-burning stove, half-again larger than the one we had in our dining room at home. Starting with cold weather that first fall, the teacher made sure the stove was going by the time the first students arrived. On top of the stove, Miss Piechowski placed a pan of water that steamed all day. Many of us brought jars of homemade soup from home, and we placed them in the steaming water a half-hour or so before noon.

Delicious smells of ten or more different kinds of soups and vegetables seeped into every corner of the room. The smells were better than those coming from the restaurant in town. Although I had never been in the restaurant, we sometimes walked by when the doors were open. The smells were everywhere, wonderful smells of food cooking and pies baking and coffee boiling. But these smells you paid for when you went inside and eased up to the counter. The food smells in the country school were free and I smelled them every day, not just once in a great while when we were in town and walking by a restaurant at mealtime.

To the right of the stove was a sink for hand washing, and a water cooler. When we wanted a drink of water at home, we walked over to the water pail in the kitchen and with the dipper ladled out what we wanted. Here was a modern convenience. When we needed a drink of water, we walked over to the cooler and pushed a little button, and water bubbled up. It took a little getting used to. The first couple of times water shot me in the nose. It ran down my chin, too, and I never could get enough. When you drink out of a dipper, you get plenty of water in your mouth. Not so with one of these fancy water coolers.

For the water cooler to work, you had to walk out to the pump house, grab the pump handle, and jerk it up and down many times to fill a water pail that you set under the spout. Then you toted the water into the schoolhouse and dumped it into the cooler. This was a duty for older pupils—Miss Piechowski called all the tasks around the school "duties". I kind of wondered why we didn't just sit the water pail by the sink. It was a lot easier drinking from a dipper and a water pail than pushing the little button and having a small stream of water squirt up your nose. But when modern things come along, it's best you try to keep up. At least that's how I reasoned what had happened.

I learned many things at Chain O' Lake School. Most important of all, I learned how to read. What a wonderful thing it is to know how to read. I soon discovered that a new world was there for me to learn about—I only had to open the pages in a book and read.

I learned some other things in first grade, too. I learned about coloring and staying within the lines, cutting out circles and triangles and staying on the line, and standing in a line when I waited to wash my hands at lunch time. I learned about numbers and telling time, and where Wisconsin, Minnesota, Iowa, Illinois, and Michigan were on the map. I learned how to print my name and several other words. In fact, by the end of first grade, I considered myself quite well educated. Of course I didn't use words like "educated." I just let folks know that I knew many things. There were lots of things I didn't know, but if you don't know what it is you don't know, how can you possibly be concerned about not knowing it?

Before first grade, one thing I didn't know about was girls. I had twin brothers. The Kolka boys, Jim and Dave, who were my best friends, had a sister, but she was old. I had had lots of experience with my mother, but she was not a girl, she was my mother. So there was no practical way to learn about girls.

One of my first serious attempts to learn about girls, beyond noticing that one was sitting across from me and another behind me in school, occurred in May. Pauline had been friendly to me all year. She was a grade ahead of me and a little taller than I was. She had black hair fixed in braids and dark eyes that smiled before her mouth did. At age five I don't recall if I knew much about who was cute and who wasn't. More important was who was friendly and who wouldn't try to steal your lunch. Pauline was surely friendly and besides that she smelled good.

I don't know how I got this idea into my head. Maybe George Jeffers suggested it—I don't recall. Anyway, I wanted to kiss Pauline. Not only did I know little about girls, I knew nothing about kissing. I'd overheard some of the older boys talking about kissing and how much fun it was. So I must have figured it was never too young to find out for yourself.

On this particularly warm May day, I had been glancing over at Pauline where she worked at her desk, trying to figure out how I might kiss her. The only personal experience I had with kissing was when my mother kissed me just before I went to bed. She always kissed me on the cheek so I figured this was a good place to start. The older boys had talked about kissing girls on the lips, but this I quickly put in the category of advanced kissing. Better learn how to kiss on the cheek before you move to more advanced levels. After all, I had seven more years of country school to work on these more lofty goals.

When school was over that day and we were out in the school yard, I asked Pauline, "Can I kiss you?"

"Could you what?" replied Pauline. She looked like someone had just dropped a frog down her back.

"Kiss you."

"No."

"Why not?"

"You're too little."

"I know how to kiss," I lied.

Pauline began running down the road toward her home, a direction different from the one to our farm.

I began running after her.

"Just one kiss on the cheek?" I yelled.

No reply.

Unfortunately, Pauline could run faster than I could, a lot faster. Before long I lost sight of her around the corner. I walked back to school. The few remaining students were snickering and poking each other. I tried to ignore them as I grabbed my empty lunch bucket and started the long walk home. I felt terrible. But I had learned a valuable lesson about girls and about kissing. Unfortunately, as the years passed I have forgotten just what that important lesson was.

I also learned what it was like to be picked on, and what you could do about it. When I was in third grade, I was easy prey for older kids who believed it was their God-given right as older, more experienced students, to pick on the littler ones. George Jeffers, tall for his age and kind of mean-looking, was a seventh-grader. He took great pride in making sure I knew my place. One of his favorite tricks was to yank the cap off my head and run with it. My cap, a blue baseball type I'd gotten for Christmas, was special. I only had one, and I wore it to school every day. I knew I would be in deep trouble if I arrived home without my cap. When I wasn't sitting at my desk in school, my cap was on my head. I wanted to make sure no one picked it up by mistake.

On this particular day, I was in the woodshed, a little building near the schoolhouse. My duty that week was to carry in kindling wood for the woodstove that heated the school building. With my cap firmly in place, I was in the woodshed loading my arms with split pine kindling wood. George Jeffers quietly slipped up behind me and snapped off my cap. He surprised me so I dropped my armful of kindling wood and yelled, "Give me back my cap, George!"

Trying to be more of a bully than he really was, George replied.

"Make me."

I may have been little, but the words "make me" snapped something inside. Before, when he had taken my cap, I had pleaded for him to give it back. Not this time. I felt anger surging through me.

I grabbed the biggest piece of kindling wood I could find and with one motion brought the wood down on George's head. He fell in a heap at my feet. Never before had I observed such a look of surprise and pain in my life.

Quickly, George struggled to his feet, dropping my cap in the process. Tears began rolling down his face and then he began bawling. It is not a pleasant thing to watch a would-be bully cry, but at that moment I thought it was the most pleasurable thing that I'd ever seen.

George ran for the school, reporting to Miss Murty, our teacher that year, that I had beaten him with a piece of kindling wood. He, of course, failed to mention that he had first stolen my cap. Miss Murty, a short, portly woman known for keeping order, sat us both down and listened to our stories. I suspected the worst. Surely a month's worth of carrying in kindling wood, two weeks of sweeping out the boys outdoor toilet, and an assignment to pound the chalk from the blackboard erasers for the rest of the school year.

In addition to being a fine teacher, Miss Murty was a better-than-average judge. After hearing testimony from both of us, she immediately offered her judgment. To George Jeffers she said,

"George, I hope you've learned your lesson. Don't steal any more caps."

"I have learned my lesson, Miss Murty," replied George.

I knew he hadn't. George could lie with a straight

face better than any other kid in school. But this was surely not the time to point out that fact especially when I hadn't yet heard what judgment would be leveled against me.

"Jerold," Miss Murty said. She always called me Jerold when matters were serious. It was an ominous sign.

"You've done a bad thing."

"I know I have, Miss Murty." I wanted to point out that if ever anyone deserved a stick over the head, it was George Jeffers. But I kept my mouth shut. Pa had always told me that when things are not going your way, keep your mouth shut; whatever you say might make matters worse.

"I don't ever want to hear that you hit anyone else with a stick of kindling wood, a baseball bat, or anything else."

"You'll never hear that again, Miss Murty."

I was waiting for the worst. First comes the judgment, then comes the sentencing. I braced myself to hear the punishment, which I knew would be severe. With both hands I held my cap in front of me. At least I still had my cap.

"There will be no punishment for either of you. From the looks of that welt on your head, George, you've been punished. Jerold, don't you ever do this again."

"I won't, Miss Murty," I said.

"Now go back outside and play. Recess will be over in five minutes."

George never again took my cap. Thus there was no cause to hit him again, with anything. I wish I had thought of the baseball bat, though. George wouldn't have gotten up so fast if I had clobbered him with that.

Other Learning

There is much that is learned outside the school-room when you live on a farm. Farm kids learn from their fathers and mothers as they work beside them doing farm chores, such as milking cows and caring for the chickens. Farm kids learn about the significance of work, the need to get up in the morning, and the importance of respect and never talking back to your parents. All of these things are learned directly from fathers and mothers.

Other things are learned that don't come from parents, at least intentionally. Learning how to cuss is one of those things. Swearing lessons were occasionally conducted at our country school, back of the boys' toilet during recess and noon breaks. The older, more experienced boys felt it their obligation as upperclassmen to pass on their superior knowledge of these matters to those who followed behind them. Of course, swearing lessons were only conducted for boys and by boys, and not for the little boys either. You had to be of a proper age, about fourth grade, before you were invited to the classes.

None of us boys knew what went on back of the girls' toilet when girls gathered there. We assumed their discussions were about dolls and other such girl topics, nothing as heady as swearing lessons. We did hear some giggles from time to time, and even saw some glances come our way. But their discussions were a mystery to us, and we assumed they knew nothing about the important education that we were receiving.

Our out-of-school education had been going well when new neighbors moved onto the farm across the field from our place.

"I just heard who bought Olson's place," Pa announced when he returned home from the gristmill

one fall afternoon.

"Who?" Ma asked. The Olsons had been good friends, our closest neighbors to the west, about three-quarters of a mile away. We could see their farm buildings when we worked near the western boundary of our farm.

"If I heard right, it's Tom and Winny Milton. They came from somewhere in the southern part of the state. Name sounds English," Pa said. Our neighborhood was a mixture of ethnic backgrounds: Norwegian, German, English, Polish, Welsh, and Bohemian all living within a few miles of each other.

"They got any kids?" my brothers and I asked in unison. The Olsons were an older couple; their daughters had married and left home many years ago, and now, in their retirement, the Olsons had moved to town. Few kids our age lived in the neighborhood, at least none within easy walking distance. Our best friends were the Kolka boys, Jim and Dave, and they lived a good mile away. The distance didn't prevent us from playing with them, but it would be fun to have some kids living closer.

"They got four boys and a girl. Two grown and gone, three boys living at home. One is just a little shaver, a year old or so. But the other two must be about the ages of you guys," Pa said.

As was the custom, the neighbors held a welcoming party for the Miltons a few weeks after they moved in. We all gathered at the Miltons' house for an evening of visiting, card playing, and eating. Everyone brought something to share: bologna sandwiches, chocolate cake, green Jell-O with bananas, dill pickles—the usual food for a neighborhood get-together.

All the kids came along no matter what their ages. My brothers and I sat at a table with two of the Milton boys, Joe and Frank. Frank was my age. Joe was several years younger. I noticed that they both needed haircuts. We began playing Old Maids. I immediately caught that they didn't talk exactly like the rest of us. It wasn't so much how they used regular words but how they used swear words. Sometimes they used so many swear words that it was hard to follow what they were saying.

It became immediately clear to me that neither of the Milton boys could say a sentence that didn't have at least one cuss word in it, and sometimes two or three. It wasn't that swearing was new to me; I'd had several years of swearing lessons out back of the school outhouse. What was different here was that the Milton boys were swearing at home. My brothers and I had long ago discovered that we didn't ever practice our newly acquired swear words at home.

One time I recall my little brother Murf either forgot or just wasn't thinking when he let a string of newly learned cusswords slip out of his mouth after he dropped a stick of stove wood on his foot. You'd think a bolt of lightning had struck Ma. Her hand went to her mouth in disbelief. She grabbed little Murf by the back of his shirt, dragged him over to the kitchen sink, and stuck a piece of hand soap in his mouth.

"Only way to shut off swear words is to wash your mouth out with soap," Ma said. I watched in horror as soap bubbled out of Murf's mouth. He looked like I imagined a mad dog would look, although I had never seen a mad dog. He was sputtering and spitting and crying all at the same time. He hadn't yet realized what he had done that was so terribly wrong to evoke this kind of severe punishment. From that time for-ward, no swear words were ever uttered within hearing distance of Ma.

Now here we were at the Miltons' house, receiving a high-level education in swearing, well beyond anything I had ever heard behind the outhouse at school. To my knowledge (and I tried to keep up on these matters) nobody at our country school had advanced to this level of swearing. For instance, we never used the word "Christ"—the "C word"—in our cussing, yet the Milton boys used it regularly, drawing out the word so that it took a great length of time to move from beginning to end when speaking it: Key-e-e-e-e-ryst. We reserved the C word for church and sometimes for table prayers, and that was all. But the C word tumbled out of the Milton boys as easily as rain drips off a roof during a rainstorm. S-O-B was pronounced in such an eloquent way as I had never heard before. I could see that my brothers were as impressed as I was. Where had the Milton boys learned how to swear like this?

The greatest surprise of all occurred when skinny Joe Milton got a bad card. Little Joe, as his folks called him, was the thinnest little guy. Grandma Witt would have taken one look at him and said, "Feed that kid. Get some meat on his bones." But Grandma Witt wasn't around anymore.

Anyway, this underfed, black-haired Milton boy uttered the F word right out loud. The F word was one of those swear words that was never, ever spoken. It was a far more powerful word than even the C word. At Chain O' Lake School, we only whispered the F word and that was on rare occasions when some of us older fellows gathered back of the boys' toilet and wanted to impress the younger boys that we were up-to-date when it came to swearing.

Not only did Little Joe utter the F word once, but twice. The second time he put the word "mother" in front of it and added the C word and the S-O-B words all in one sentence. This was clearly the pinnacle of swearing and probably deserved some distinctive recognition among those who respected people with special skills.

I knew now that the Milton boys would be treated with the utmost respect at our country school during recess and noon break. They would immediately take over that lofty position of instructors in swearing.

My brothers and I were so busy playing Old Maid and learning new swear words and how to string them together in sentences that we didn't notice Ma had been listening in for the past several minutes. I was sure that she had heard the sentence in which the F word, the mother-F word, the S-O-B words, and the C word were all strung together with special emphasis put on each. She had that struck-by-lightning look that I remembered when Murf had let go a couple of swear words and had his mouth washed out with soap for the trouble. This time, though, Ma looked like she had been twice struck by lightning, for she was gasping and trying to gain some semblance of composure.

Someone announced it was time for lunch and we immediately stopped playing cards and got in line. I saw that Ma was whispering something to Pa as he heaped his plate with sandwiches, Jell-O, and two kinds of cake.

We had no more than cleaned our plates when Ma said it was time to go. I said that no one else was going yet, but she had a certain tone to her voice that meant we were leaving right away.

I don't imagine we were down the road more than

a few hundred feet when Ma said, "I have never heard such swearing in my life."

Pa had a little grin on his face because he had seen Ma worked up over little things like this before, at least Pa considered them little things.

"I don't want my boys to have a thing to do with those Milton boys," she spit out with such disdain that I figured there was little give in her decision.

Pa didn't answer for awhile. Then he said quietly, "Don't forget, Ma, they are our neighbors."

For Pa, being a neighbor was a special responsibility, and caring for neighbors was important no matter what character blemishes might be a part of their make-up. But for my brothers and me, other thoughts were taking center stage. We couldn't wait until the following Monday, when the Milton kids would start school. There surely would be a major fight when George Jeffers, who prided himself in up-to-date swearing, was confronted by the Milton boys and their unique skills. In addition to all this new learning about swearing, maybe we'd learn something new about fighting.

Party Line

The wooden telephone, with a black receiver hanging on its side and a black and silver mouthpiece sticking out its front, hung on the east wall of the dining room, at a height comfortable for Pa but too high for Ma, who had to stand on her tiptoes to speak into it. Six of our neighbors were also on our line. You knew when someone was calling by the number and length of the rings. Our ring was a long ring and three short rings. The Milton's ring was three short rings. Coswells, who lived across from the Miltons, could be reached with a long and two shorts.

It didn't matter whether the call was for you or not; whenever the phone rang you ran for the telephone to listen in. It was one way for farm people to find out what was going on in the community. If Ma was in the house, which was most of the time, she answered the telephone when it rang our ring or lis-tened in when someone else called. Occasionally we got a long-distance call, usually from a relative. We could always tell when it was long distance because Ma would whisper "long distance," and she would then begin yelling into the telephone mouthpiece. The farther away the caller lived, the louder Ma fig-ured she had to yell in order to be heard.

My brothers and I were not to use the telephone, not to answer it, not to call from it, and, above all, never to listen in on other people's calls.

Mrs. Coswell was fun to listen in on, which my brothers and I did when Ma was outside and we hap-pened to be in the house when the phone rang. Mrs. Coswell called Mrs. Handrich when the Miltons did something she didn't approve of. This occurred every day, sometimes more than once a day, for there was little that the Miltons did that Mrs. Coswell thought

worthy of overlooking.

The Miltons, besides being masters of profanity, had other quirks that added spice to the neighborhood. Tom and Winny Milton didn't get along all that well, and Mrs. Coswell was often witness to loud yelling and threats that the Miltons made to each other.

One day in December we heard Handrich's ring, and Ma trotted off to listen in. Soon she began smiling and then laughing aloud. As she laughed, she tried to keep her right hand planted firmly over the mouthpiece, so no one would know she was listening. She might as well have kept her right hand in her apron pocket, for everyone on the party line listened and everyone knew that they did.

Later Ma told us—she had trouble repeating the story she was laughing so hard—that Tom and Winny had gotten into a terrible fight. In the middle of the altercation, Winny picked up a huge piece of stove wood and heaved it straight at Tom's head. He ducked and the block of wood busted through their dining-room window and landed in a snowbank outside their house.

"Now I don't know how Mrs. Coswell found all this out, but you know Mrs. Coswell, she is about as nosy as they come, and if there is something to find out, she'd find it," Ma said.

Ma offered that one of the Milton kids probably told Mrs. Coswell, complete with the words that each combatant spoke and at what point the block of wood was taken up and heaved.

Ma, laughing so that now there were tears in her eyes, continued to share the tale.

"Mrs. Coswell said that after the block of wood sailed through the dining-room window, the fighting came to an abrupt halt. I suspect when that blast of cold air shot into the dining room they both cooled off." Ma sat down before she could continue. "Before you could say 'A block of wood just smashed through the dining-room window,' old Tom was outside with a pillow off their bed, stuffing it in the hole to keep out the cold.

"I wonder what'll be next," Ma said, as she took a deep breath and wiped the tears away with her handkerchief.

Another time, when we were eating supper, the

phone rang Handrich's ring and Ma pushed back her chair and hurried into the dining room to listen in.

Pa, my brothers, and I kept on eating, listening to Ma giggle occasionally as she took in another tale of the life of the Miltons and their continued antagonism of straight-laced Mrs. Coswell, who spent most waking hours gazing across the road. This time, Ma related when she returned to the table, the littlest Milton boy had been running up and down the gravel road in front of the Coswell house without a stitch of clothing on his back. He was wearing his shoes though, because the road had been freshly graveled and there were some sharp stones.

"Mrs. Coswell thinks that old lady Milton put the kid up to the trick," Ma said.

"I think she's got it right," Pa offered as we continued eating supper, with our thoughts, for a moment at least, away from low-priced milk, a sick cow, and rain that seemed never to come.

But the party-line telephone had another important role besides providing humor for the community. On a warm evening in April, when the grass was just beginning to green up by the cellar door, and the pond frogs had begun to call, the phone nearly leaped off the wall. It was a series of short rings, five or six, a brief pause, and then another series of short rings. A general ring it was called, and no one wanted to hear it because it meant someone was in trouble. Ma hurried to the phone and lifted the receiver off the hook.

"The Hoover Jenks' barn is on fire and they need help," Central said when the ringing stopped briefly. Everyone called the telephone operator who sat behind the switchboard in town "Central".

The ringing continued for fifteen minutes or so, an ominous sound. As soon as Ma heard the message, she hurried out to the barn to tell Pa and me. We stopped milking, ran for the car, and drove to the Jenks' farm about three miles from our place. It was early evening, and a few streaks of sunlight still played on the western horizon.

What we saw when we arrived at the Jenks' farm was what no farmer ever wanted to see. Flames shot from under the roof of the barn, orange and red flames that sent a gigantic cloud of black smoke skyward. Cars pulled into the yard from all directions. Farmers, some of them with red handkerchiefs tied over their mouths, rushed back and forth from the pump house to the flaming barn. The village volunteer fire department wouldn't leave the village, said they didn't have insurance for fighting country fires. So farmers depended on their neighbors. Barns were almost never saved once they caught fire. Usually, with some luck and no wind, the farmhouse and some of the other outbuildings could be spared from the flames.

I noticed that most of the farmers were tossing water on the machine shed, which was only a few yards from the barn. The building was steaming and sizzling, but so far the farmers and their water pails were winning.

The bawling of the cattle trapped in the barn troubled me most. I knew normal cattle sounds, but these sounds I had not heard before. These were sounds of terror, as cattle faced death from the encroaching smoke and flames.

"Pa, who's helping get the cows out?" I yelled.

"Nobody," he answered, wiping a hand over his smoke-stained face.

"Why not?"

"It's no use. Fire's too hot. Besides, the smoke will kill them before they burn. It won't be so bad."

After a while the bawling stopped, and I knew the cows were dead. Soon the fire was down to a flaming pile of hay. The rest of the building had been consumed. Farmers began leaving; most of them had evening chores left to finish at home.

Hoover Jenks (his real first name was Alfred but everyone called him Hoover) stood near the pump house, his red face covered with soot and a burn hole in his shirt. Hoover was thanking everyone for coming. Neighbors, in turn, said how they wished they could have done more to save his barn and his cows.

Pa stopped to shake his hand and offered to help him any way that he could. Faith, Hoover's wife, stood off to the side, crying, wondering if they had enough money to build another barn and buy some more cows.

"Good thing we all had telephones," Pa said.

Chicken Dance

A block of wood stood out back of the chicken house, the end piece of an oak tree. It was maybe two feet tall and a foot-and-a-half across. Two nails about an inch and a half apart had been pounded part way into the top of the block. Most of the time the block just sat there, a mystery to those who didn't know the ways of the country and how things got done using equipment that seemed a mite unorthodox.

In early November, sometimes as early as late October if the weather had been cool, Ma would announce at the breakfast table that it was time to butcher chickens. Depending on the amount of money Pa had to buy baby chicks back in the spring, we either butchered some plump, tender, and wide-breasted Plymouth Rock broilers, or we captured and killed some Leghorn laying hens that were narrow of breast and were sometimes as tough as an old shoe.

We only butchered Leghorns that no longer laid eggs, which meant some were several years old. The Plymouth Rock broilers were only a few months old and far more tender than the worn-out laying hens.

Butchering day was something my brothers and I looked forward to, mostly I suspect, because it broke the routine of daily chores, such as carrying wood and water, feeding the pigs, and helping in the barn. Messy as it was, butchering chickens was interesting and without equal. You might say it resembled hog butchering, but you'd be wrong in that assumption. Killing a pig and killing a chicken are about as different as sawing down an oak tree and chopping off a corn stalk.

On this particular Saturday, two city cousins were visiting. My brothers and I looked forward to introducing them to the ritual of chicken butchering and all its blood and gore, smells and mess. Ronny and Bob didn't know much about the ways of the farm because they had spent much of their lives in Chicago. In the best possible way, we prepared them for the event, telling them that they would be splattered with blood, would see things that would turn their stomachs, and would smell things they wish they hadn't smelled. It was near Halloween so it seemed altogether appropriate that we painted the most wicked and monstrous picture of the process of ending chickens' lives.

Right after breakfast, my brothers carried several pails of water in from the pump house and filled the copper boiler that Ma had put on the hottest part of the woodstove. Boiling water was an important part of chicken butchering, but when cousin Ron asked how we would use the water, I answered, in the most mysterious voice I could muster, "You'll find out soon enough."

While the water was coming to a boil on the stove, Pa was out in the chicken house, sorting out the hens. By the time I'd gotten there you'd think a fox had sneaked into the chicken house. Chickens were running around, feathers were flying, and there was so much squawking and clucking that I couldn't talk loud enough for Pa to hear. I knew about chicken butchering, knew it well, but I didn't know chicken sorting. Pa was grabbing up the skinny Leghorns, one at a time, tipping them up and looking at their bottom ends. He could tell which ones were laying and which ones were on vacation by a quick glance, and I wanted to find out how. A wire chicken crate stood on the floor in the corner. About every third or fourth chicken he inspected he shoved in the chicken crate after sliding back the wire door. When I arrived, four hens were already in the crate. These were the doomed birds, the chickens destined for soup and other chicken recipes that my mother knew so well.

I stood alongside Pa while he made his quick inspections. Even though I watched his every movement, I never did figure out exactly what he was looking for. I also wondered how many innocent birds—those that were still laying—would be condemned because Pa had seen something that wasn't there, whatever it was. Ma reminded him of his mistakes because she found out for sure which hens were laying and which ones were not when she pulled out their insides, her part of the butchering process. She knew by the partially formed eggs she found inside that a bird was laying.

Soon there were a dozen hens in the chicken crate.

"Grab that side," Pa said.

Together we carried the crate full of chickens out back of the chicken house, near the chopping block with the two nails pounded into the top. Here stood my two city cousins and my brothers, waiting patiently for the most gruesome part of butchering. Bob, the younger of my cousins, had been listening to my brothers tell

him about how awful would be the sight, and how the shrieks of the dying birds would be next to unbearable, and that he would probably want to run for the house the first time a chicken screamed. Of course I knew, and my brothers knew too, that these were all lies. Chickens do not scream when they are killed. About the only sound you get out of a chicken about to die is a soft cluck or sometimes a cackle, but nothing that comes close to a death scream.

My brother's story was working. My little cousin's eyes were as big as pie plates as he stood taking it all in. Murf had a big smirk on his face—he couldn't hold it back anymore—and Duck, well, he just continued laying it on. Once you got a pushover, he figured, you took him for all you could.

All talk stopped when we sat the chicken crate with the doomed chickens next to the chopping block. Earlier, Pa had sharpened the hatchet blade. He now grabbed up the hatchet and said to me, "Hand me one of those hens."

It was a beautiful fall Saturday. The sun was up full in a clear blue sky. The oak woods just beyond the chicken house were awash in color—deep browns, reds, tans, orange-browns, yellow-browns, every shade of brown you could imagine. But no one was looking at the fall colors or the blue, sun-filled sky. All eyes were on me as I slid back the wire door and fished around in the chicken crate until I grabbed the leg of a hen and pulled her out. Quickly, I handed the chicken to Pa, who in one nonstop motion stuck her head between the two nails on the block, pulled on her neck until it was tight, lifted the hatchet over his head, and brought it down with a "thuck." The severed head fell on the ground and he tossed the bird aside. Immediately the headless chicken jumped to its feet and began running round in tight little circles, blood flying everywhere.

"The chicken's doing a death dance," said brother Murf, for the benefit of his cousins, especially the younger one.

"Ain't it fun to see it dance," Murf said, laughing.

"Gimme another hen," Pa ordered. And I went digging in the crate for another chicken. Soon two headless chickens were dancing, and then three. Somehow, they avoided bumping into each other as they did their ballet.

Cousin Bob's face had turned white, and he looked like he was going to throw up. He let out a little gasp and ran for the house. He had apparently seen enough. It wasn't the death screams of the birds that had gotten to him, but the fact that a chicken without its head could still run around for a minute or so, as if its head was still in place. Nobody had told him about this part of butchering chickens. Surprise is always important when you're trying to scare somebody. And the system had worked.

"Gimme another hen," Pa said. In the chicken butchering process there is no time for squeamish relatives. The work had to go on. Cousin Ron remained. He was older, and he knew he would never hear the end of it if he also ran to the house. With each butchered chicken his face got whiter, but he stayed until the last chicken danced.

Pa, my brothers, and I gathered up the headless chickens, now dead in the dust, and carried them to a little opening near the woods. I ran to the house and brought out a pail of boiling water and a pan for the cleaned chickens. On my way back, I walked slowly and carefully so as not to spill any water on my leg.

Pa grabbed a dead hen by its legs and shoved it into the boiling water, sloshed it up and down a few times, and then handed the soggy bird to Murf who knew that his job was to yank off the wet feathers, revealing a skinny, naked, former laying hen. Watching the blood fly and the dead chicken dancing was the worst of the killing part of butchering. Smelling dead feathers was the worst of chicken plucking. Nothing—not drying wet wool, not rotten potatoes (well, maybe a rotten egg)—equaled the smell of wet chicken feathers.

The next chicken was mine to pluck, and the next one went to Duck, and so on. Cousin Ron just stood there, white-faced, holding his nose. Soon the dozen yellowish, naked birds lay in a heap in a wash basin. Ma was ready in the house for the final step in the process, pulling out the insides. She saved the liver, heart, and gizzard, delicacies that we all enjoyed.

Cousin Bob thought he'd like to watch Ma pull out chicken guts, but he didn't realize that a special strong smell went along with the process. Soon he rushed out of the kitchen, onto the back porch. Was there any place for a city cousin where the smells and sights of chicken butchering could be avoided?

Before the end of the day, the chickens had been cleaned, cut into pieces, and shoved into canning jars for processing. On a cold winter's day, Ma would retrieve one of the jars and make a huge kettle of chicken soup. No one thought of butchering day while we ate, but we often talked about how our cousins had reacted.

Rainy Day

There was always work on the farm, and no vacations. We talked about people who had vacations, including some of our relatives who lived in cities. But anyone who didn't work every day, especially in summer, was "on the lazy order" to Pa's way of thinking. We even worked Sundays, though not as much—just milked the cows, cared for the chickens, and did the other work that had to be done every day of year.

Rainy days were sometimes different. On a rainy day, especially an unsettled day when you didn't know if it was going to pour rain, quit raining, or maybe just drizzle a little, we went fishing. Fishing meant no fences to fix and no thistles to hoe in the cornfield. No weeding in the garden and no sacking corn for a trek to the gristmill.

I recall one such day. I was eleven, my twin brothers, seven. Rain had fallen most of the night, a slow, steady, soaking rain. The kind of rain that makes corn grow and keeps pastures green and alive. The kind of rain that sandy-soil farmers hope will fall about once a week, but are lucky to see once a month during the middle days of summer.

After we'd milked the cows, turned them out of the barn, and slipped the full milk cans into the water-filled cooling tank, we sat around the kitchen table finishing breakfast.

"Oughta go fishin' today," Pa said. "Ain't been fishin' much this summer. Course it ain't rained much either."

These were the words my brothers and I wanted to hear. I ran for the cane poles tucked under the eaves of the corncrib where they were out of the weather. Each fishing pole was about 16 feet long and was wrapped with 24 or so feet of heavy green fishing line. A good cane-pole fisherman figured the line should be about one-and-a-half times longer than the pole. Any longer than that and you might have the line wrapped around your neck when you tried to toss it out in the lake; any shorter and you were short-changing the possibility of getting your hook out where the big ones lived.

Back of the chicken house, Pa, the twins, and I dug angleworms with a six-tine barn fork. Here was a patch of fertile soil that the chickens kept free of weeds and grass and that the rain off the chicken house roof kept moist.

"Duck, you pick 'em up while I dig," Pa said. Duck held a discarded

pork and beans can in his left hand. He grabbed up the fat worms with his right hand. Sometimes as many as four or five emerged from each forkful of soil that Pa turned.

Murf and I kept track of the count—ten, twenty. When we got to fifty, Pa said, "That oughta do it."

With a hard tug Pa checked the line on each of the four fishing poles and made sure each had a cork and a hook. Fishing line, corks, and hooks were available in Hotz's Hardware Store in Wild Rose. Mr. Hotz was a member of the Methodist church, and when you bought hooks, he packaged them in Methodist church donation envelopes. I never found out if he got unused envelopes from the church or merely didn't attend very often and had lots left over. It was none of my business. What I knew was the little donation envelopes made fine hook containers.

With binder twine, Duck and I tied the bamboo poles over the top of the '36 Plymouth, skinny ends to the front. Before tying them we wrapped a gunny bag around the poles so they wouldn't scratch the old black Plymouth's roof anymore than it was already marred.

"Let's try Norwegian Lake," Pa said. We had several choices. Occasionally, we fished Round Lake or

Bean's Lake, and when we visited my Uncle Ed we fished Gilbert Lake because it was near where he lived. But Norwegian Lake was Pa's favorite for summer fishing—there were other choices for winter.

Norwegian Lake offered an assortment of fish—better than average size bluegills, sunfish, and crappies, big bullheads with long whiskers, thick heads, and leathery black skin, and huge northern pike. At least that's what I thought they were. It was not uncommon to hook a northern that weighed five pounds or more. Some fishermen caught northerns twice or three times that size, but I had never been that lucky and wasn't sure I wanted one of those monsters lurching around while I held a cane pole. On cloudy days or when the sun was just going down and the bullfrogs were beginning to call, we sometimes caught bass among the lily pads close to shore.

Today we were after bluegills. "Sweetest tasting fish there is," Pa said. "Not even trout tastes as sweet as a bluegill."

We drove the seven or eight miles to Norwegian Lake and pulled into Anderson's farmyard on the west end of the lake. It was difficult to fish Norwegian Lake from shore, too much marshland. To fish the lake well, you needed a boat, and Ted Anderson rented boats.

Pa handed Mrs. Anderson a dollar bill.

"Hope you have good luck, Herman," she said.

"I think we will," Pa replied.

We grabbed up a pair of oars from Anderson's wagon shed before driving down the narrow wagon trail to the boat landing. The boat landing consisted of a short wooden dock that leaned toward the east so that one side was mostly under water. Four wooden boats, all half filled with water from the recent rain, were tied to the dock.

"Pick out a good one," Pa said as he gestured toward the boats. None of them looked exceptional, especially when they were mostly submerged. I picked out one with three seats. The back seat was big enough for my brothers, I could sit in the front seat, and Pa would sit in the middle and row.

I started bailing water from the boat with an old rusty pail that was likely there for that purpose. Soon the boat was floating. We loaded our gear and everyone crawled in.

"Sit down, you guys, and don't move. This boat ain't all that steady," Pa said as he slipped the oars into the oarlocks and began rowing toward the middle of the lake.

"You can start unwinding your fishing poles and get ready," he said as the boat slowly moved across the lake's smooth surface. The oars made a gurgling sound in the water and left little swirls when Pa lifted them. I began twisting my cane pole, allowing the thick green fishing line to play out in the water; my brothers did the same with their poles. Soon we arrived at Pa's favorite fishing spot in the lake, a place where we could anchor the boat in three or four feet of water and yet fish a few yards away in water so deep it was inky black as far as you stared into it.

"Big fish in the deep water this time of year," Pa said as he slipped a concrete-filled pail—the anchor—over the side with a splash.

Soon four corks were bobbing on the water, fat angleworms wiggling on each hook. The drizzly rain had stopped, but the sky remained heavy and gray. I saw a mother duck swimming in the rushes near shore, six baby ducks strung out behind her in a straight line. Beyond the ducks I saw a blue heron standing knee-deep in the shallow water, not moving, waiting for an unsuspecting fish to come by, at which time, in a flash, the long-legged bird would stab the fish with its beak.

Murf was also watching the ducks.

"Where's your bobber, Murf?" Duck asked.

Murf jerked his head around and yanked the heavy bamboo pole into the air. A saucer-sized bluegill flopped on the end of the line, making an arc toward the boat where it landed with a thud at Pa's feet.

"Good one, Murf," Pa said.

"Caught the first fish," Murf said. "Got the first one." A big smile spread across his face. He dragged the flopping fish toward him, and slipped it off the hook and onto the fish stringer.

"See that?" Murf said, jabbing his finger at his twin brother. "I beat you. Got the first fish."

"Ya, ya," Duck said, trying unsuccessfully to ignore his twin.

Soon a half dozen more bluegills joined the first one on the stringer as each of us caught fish. That is,

all except Murf.

"So what happened to you, Murf?" Duck said. "Lost your touch?" No answer from his twin brother.

At that moment, Murf's bobber sank beneath the surface and continued sinking. The tip of the long fishing pole bent until it touched the water.

"Got a big one on! Got a big one on," yelled Murf, holding onto his pole with both hands as tightly as he could.

"Hooked a northern," Pa said matter of factly. "Looks like a good one. A real pole bender."

"What do I do? What do I do?" Murf yelled.

"Take it easy. Keep the line tight and let him wear down," Pa suggested.

"He's off! He's off!" Murf said. "See? The line's gone limp."

Then the line tightened and the pole began bending once more.

"I'd better pull up the anchor," Pa said. "Give that fish a little more room to play."

Slowly the boat moved in the direction of the line.

"Bet it's a ten-pounder," Murf said excitedly. "Don't have to catch a lot of fish if you catch a big one."

We waited several minutes with nothing happening.

"Pull your pole in enough so I can grab the line," Pa said. Once he had the line, he began pulling it in, hand over hand.

"Thought for a minute the fish took the line down in the weeds and let go, but it's jerking again. Never felt anything like this before. Must be a mighty big fish to jerk like this," Pa said with an excited edge to his voice.

We all stared into the black depths of the deep water, each hoping to be the first to glimpse the huge fish we knew was there. Slowly, something began to come into view. It was big and black and round and there was moss growing on one side of it. And its neck was stretched out straight.

"What is it?" I whispered, fearing that whatever creature it was might hear me.

"Big old snapping turtle," Pa said with disgust. The turtle now came into view alongside the boat. It was as big as a washtub, more than three feet across, with gruesome-looking, scale-covered legs sticking out of each corner and a mean-looking head with beady eyes on its front end.

"What do we do now?" I asked, wondering if Pa planned to hoist the big turtle into the boat.

"Only one thing to do. Cut the line and let it go. We don't want that thing in the boat with us. Turtles are mean, and this one looks mad. Course, can't really blame him—we've been yanking him around for the last fifteen minutes."

Pa reached in his pocket, took out his pocketknife, and cut the line. Slowly the big snapper settled deeper and deeper into the water until we couldn't see it anymore.

With the turtle adventure now a part of our fish story collection, Pa rowed us back to shore and we drove home. For supper that night we feasted on bluegills. Pa had a way of cleaning them where he scraped off the scales on each side, cut off the heads, and pulled out the innards, leaving the tail. Ma dipped the cleaned fish in flour and placed them in a sizzling frying pan until they were brown on both sides. To eat them you lifted an entire side of the fish

away from the backbone, leaving only a few bones to contend with. Bluegills were truly the sweetest fish you'd ever eat. It was hard telling when we'd go fishing again, so we took our time eating.

Dietrich

Grandpa Witt died in 1941, and his farm saw a series of renters all through World War II. In 1946, Pa, who looked after the place, put it up for sale. The farm included 120 hilly and stony acres, not different from other farms in the neighborhood. The farm buildings consisted of a big red barn with a silo inside and a granary built into one end, a pump house, wagon shed, and a well-kept farmhouse with five bedrooms.

In March 1947, Pa received a letter from the Dietrichs who had seen an ad for the Witt farm in a Milwaukee newspaper. They inquired about prices and details: How large was the house and how modern was it? Typical city-people questions. A couple of weeks later the Dietrichs visited the farm, liked it, and wrote Pa a check for $200 toward the $5,000 asking price.

George and Clara Dietrich had both been born and raised in Milwaukee. They had two children—Tom, nine, and Jimmy, six. George Dietrich had worked during the war years for the A. O. Smith Company. He had never set foot on a farm; neither had his wife nor their two children. But something about farm life drew them to the country.

George was a tall, thin fellow, almost frail looking. His face was chalky-white, evidence of having spent many years working inside. He also had a moustache, a thin line of hair that stretched along the top of his upper lip and jumped up and down when he talked. That single characteristic, a moustache, immediately set him off from everyone in the neighborhood. No one said it aloud, but everyone knew that men with moustaches were shifty and not to be trusted.

The Dietrichs moved in, and George immediately set out to farm. Dietrich had read many books and magazines, especially material about how to farm in the modern way. He soon let his neighbors know that although he had never lived on a farm and had never worked on one, he knew about farming, especially modern-day farming. Ask him a question about plant varieties or dairy cattle breeds, and he had a quick answer. Ask him about proper tillage approaches and he had a response. He was a font of wisdom about farming, or so it seemed. He appeared surprised that his neighbors seemed less informed than he was about the "modern ways"—after all, they had been farmers for many years.

Unfortunately, Dietrich had book answers, but practical answers were in short supply. In most instances, he didn't even know what questions to ask. Upon settling in on his new farm, Dietrich saw an ad in the *Waushara Argus* for milk cows. Without asking for assistance from Pa or anyone else, he bought the entire herd of fifteen animals. They weren't off the truck more than a couple hours when Dietrich called and asked Pa to stop by to see his new cows and offer an opinion on his good judgment in cow buying. Pa asked me to come along, which I gladly did.

We stepped into the barn and saw the most motley looking collection of milk cows I had ever seen. A couple of them were Jerseys, skinny critters with hipbones and ribs sticking out. Pa later said they looked like somebody stretched some hide over a bunch of bones. Four or five were mostly Holstein, but it was difficult to tell because they obviously were of mixed parentage. The rest of them appeared to be Guernseys, at least they were the color of Guernseys—white and reddish brown. They were a sorrowful bunch of cows.

"What do you think, Herman?" Dietrich asked, motioning toward the cows now busy eating hay from the manger in front of them. I couldn't take my eyes off Dietrich's little moustache that jumped all around when he talked.

Pa took off his cap and carefully walked the alleyway behind the cows. He ran his hand over his head, something I had seen him do before when he was placed in a delicate situation and didn't quite know how to respond. The look on Pa's face was a combination of humor and surprise. Here was a man who had read all the books and informed everyone who would listen that he knew all about milk cows and how to pick out good ones.

"Looks like most of 'em are milking," Pa said.

"They're all supposed to be," Dietrich replied.

Pa avoided answering the question. What could you say good about such a bad bunch of cows?

"Herman, I've got a problem."

"What's that?" Pa said.

"I've never milked a cow before, and the book I've got isn't too clear on how to do it. I tried to follow the directions—squeeze and pull, squeeze and pull—but nothing happens. In fact, that red and white cow didn't like it at all. She tried to kick me."

I had to cover my mouth with my hand so Dietrich wouldn't see me laughing. Here he had a barn full of cows that would have to be milked in a few hours, and he didn't know how to milk.

"I was wondering if you'd take a minute to show me how to milk— what kind of grip I ought to use, how hard I should pull," Dietrich said.

Now I really did have trouble not laughing. I turned and walked to the end of the row of cows so

Dietrich wouldn't see me.

Even Pa was grinning when he said, "It'll take a little longer than a minute, George."

"How am I going to learn?"

I could see Pa scratching his head and thinking about a problem that he'd never before confronted.

"Jerold, come on over here," Pa finally said.

I couldn't imagine what he wanted. I was still trying to keep from hooting.

"George, if Jerold is willing to do it, I'll let him stay with you folks and show you how to milk. Of course, you'll have to feed him and give him a bed and make sure he gets off to school in the morning."

The situation immediately shifted from humorous to serious. I was supposed to show this city fellow how to milk a cow, this guy with the little mustache that jiggled up and down when he talked, and who read all the farming publications but didn't know how to do the simple stuff like milking a cow.

I was attending Chain O' Lake School, and it was a mile walk to school from the home farm. From Grandpa's farm it was more than two-and-a-half miles, but I'd be walking with the Kolka boys and they knew a trail through the woods that made the trip a little shorter.

I looked at Pa and then at Mr. Dietrich.

"I'll do it," I said. The look on Pa's face suggested I didn't have much of a choice. Pa wanted Dietrich to succeed. If he lost the farm, then Pa would have to sell it again.

After supper, Pa brought me back to Dietrich's farm, along with some extra clothes and my school books. Dietrich and I immediately walked out to the pump house, grabbed a couple milk pails and a milk can, and walked on to the barn.

As we walked, I was wondering how I would teach Dietrich how to milk his scraggly cows. I was trying to think how I had learned. You don't just follow a series of steps and then you've got the technique. But what do you do? It was something like tying your shoes. When you know how to do it, you know how to do it, and you have a dickens of a time trying to show someone else how.

Once in the barn, I asked which cow he wanted to milk first.

"How about this one?" he said.

He pointed to a homely Guernsey-Holstein cross, blackish-red in color. Half of one horn sloped down while the other horn pointed up, giving her head a kind of unbalanced look. She was one of the worst-looking cows I had ever seen.

"What do I do, Jerold?"

I looked around, spotted a three-legged milk stool hanging on the barn wall, and handed it to Dietrich.

"Put the milk stool by the cow and sit down."

"Which side?"

"Right side when you're standing behind the cow. Most cows are milked on the right side. If you crawl in on the other side, she'll probably kick your head off."

Dietrich sat down on the stool and I handed him a milk pail.

"Now put this milk pail between your knees and squeeze the pail just enough so it won't drop on the floor."

Dietrich seemed eager to learn, even from a kid. I was beginning to see another side to this man with the moustache and a head full of farm book knowledge.

"Now you see those four tits?" I said.

"You mean teats?" Dietrich corrected me.

"We always called them tits. Grab one in each hand and start squeezing."

Milk cows might look dumb, and homely ones might even look dumber, but a milk cow knows when somebody is yanking on her tits and doesn't know what he's doing. You only have to look at a cow's ears, watch her back legs, and see what she does with her tail. If she begins to shuffle her back legs a little, look out. She's giving you fair warning that something is not right and you can expect a more serious reaction. If her wire-haired tail begins flailing the air when there are no flies around, you're in for some real trouble. But some cows do this all the time. They just don't like being milked. In this case, I figured this old brindle cow was reacting to a novice milker.

"How's it going?" I asked.

"It's not," Dietrich answered. "Haven't got a drop of milk." Sweat was pouring from Dietrich's face as he squeezed and squeezed.

"Here, let me try," I said.

To her advantage, this cow had big tits, the kind you grab hold of and use your whole hand while milk-ing. Some younger cows had such little tits that you had to use your thumb and first finger. I gave the tit a squeeze and a big stream of chalky-white milk hit the bottom of the pail with a loud "zing." It surprised Dietrich so he almost dropped the pail. I repeated the process three or four times.

"Now, you try it," I suggested.

Dietrich grabbed the same tit from which I had just gotten milk and squeezed with all his might. His face grew red, and the cow began to fidget.

Any second I expected her to kick and send Dietrich, the milk pail, and the stool flying into the aisle. But this old cow had an uncommon level of tol-erance.

Sweat continued pouring from Dietrich's face as he squeezed and squeezed, but nothing happened.

"How'd you do that?"

I showed him again. "It isn't how hard you squeeze, but how you squeeze," I said. "Start your squeeze at the top of the tit, then move downward."

I shot three or four more streams of milk into the pail.

"Cow's an easy milker," I said. The moment the

words left my mouth I knew I shouldn't have said them. She was surely not an easy milker for Dietrich. He couldn't get a single drop from her.

"Ouch," Dietrich said, in a voice loud enough to cause the cow to jump, nearly upsetting him.

"What happened, cow step on your foot?" About once a week one of the cows I milked at home planted her big clawed foot on my foot, not a pleasant occurrence even for the most experienced milker.

"Nah, I hurt my hand," Dietrich said.

I wondered how the cow could hurt his hand. Had she stepped on it? I'd never seen that happen. Dietrich showed me his hand. The back of it was purplish and beginning to swell.

"I've got to run cold water over it. First-aid book says cold water is necessary for this kind of injury," Dietrich said. He handed me the milk pail and stool.

Later I learned that Dietrich had broken a blood vessel in his hand. He had squeezed so hard a big blood vessel in the back of his hand popped. I spent the rest of the week milking all of Dietrich's cows, both night and morning. Dietrich, with his hand in a huge bandage, stood watching me, hoping he'd gain some pointers on how to milk his cows. Trying to learn how to milk by watching somebody is in the same category as trying to learn how to swim by watching a swimmer. You've got to get in the water. You've got to get under a cow.

By week's end, Dietrich had purchased a mechanical milking machine, and as far as I know, he never did learn how to milk cows by hand.

Homemade Tractor

Pa had a letter from the County Agricultural Agent saying he was eligible to buy a new tractor, but there just weren't any because of the war. The demand was too great, and the number of tractors too small.

One day Pa stopped at Jim Colligan's shop in Wild Rose. Colligan was a welder-blacksmith, a kind of jack-of-all-trades who repaired farm equipment, sharpened plow points, and welded things together. Colligan wasn't a big man, not as tall as Pa, but he had the broadest shoulders I'd ever seen and the thickest arms. He was an inventor of sorts, cobbling together old things to make new things. Pa and Jim had been friends for many years—they had known each other since they were kids. They talked about the shortage of farm tractors.

"Been thinking about making a tractor," Jim said.

"How might you do that?" Pa asked.

"Well," Jim said. "Chet Hansel just bought himself a new truck and his old Model A Ford truck is still in pretty good shape. I was thinking of making a tractor out of it."

And that's what he did. He shortened the truck's frame. In place of regular truck tires, he acquired a pair of huge old tires that the county had discarded from one of its snowplows. Colligan bolted these tires to the truck wheels and left them flat, to provide more traction for the tractor. With some sheet metal, he fashioned a hood to cover the engine, and he made a seat for the operator to sit on. He covered the whole thing with aluminum paint and drove it out to the farm one summer day in 1942.

What a beauty. I was eight years old and knew I was surely not old enough to drive this fine machine.

But right then I looked forward to riding on it, along with my father.

Pa climbed on and made a couple of spins around the farmyard grinning like a Cheshire cat that had just caught a bumblebee. This was the first time he'd ever owned a tractor. Ever. He never showed much emotion, but this day it was obvious that he looked forward to sitting on this tractor and plowing, cutting grain, disking, and dragging. The tractor would make these tasks much easier compared to driving horses. Since he was a young lad, he had followed behind a team, usually walking as the team pulled a plow, a disk, or a drag. Now he could ride, and he would be ahead of the dust for a change, rather than walking in it. This was particularly true when working with a sixteen-foot-wide drag used to smooth ground before planting. The drag teeth, only three or four inches long, stirred up a considerable dust, particularly if the soil happened to be a little dry. Our sandy farm was usually dry, so dust was a part of many farm operations.

Though the tractor was truly wonderful and would soon have a great influence on how we farmed, it had its faults. The mechanical brakes were not good. It took great strength to push the brake pedal enough to engage them, particularly if the tractor happened to be on a rather steep hill. The tractor's transmission was, of course, a truck's transmission. Tractors must move only two or three miles per hour when doing heavy jobs like plowing, pulling rocks, or disking. The transmission had four speeds. Dual low, low, second, and high. Only dual low was slow enough and powerful enough for farm work. In high gear, the former truck reached speeds of forty-five or fifty miles an hour. With the larger than normal tires on the back, the machine moved even faster. Pa laid down the law early. "Whoever drives this tractor will never, ever, put it in high gear. You'll kill yourself and probably somebody else." At the moment, he was talking to himself since he was the only person on the farm who knew how to drive this new invention.

Second gear was also too fast for farm work, but might occasionally be used to drive to and from the fields, if the person was careful. Low was too fast for any heavy farm work, but could be used for such light jobs as toting an empty wagon or maybe pulling a drag.

Early in the fall, Pa hooked the tractor to his new David Bradley double-bottomed plow. It plowed two twelve-inch furrows at a time. The tractor's four-cylinder engine purred as ribbons of freshly turned soil stretched across the twenty-acre field.

"Works like a charm," Pa said that night when he drove the shiny silver tractor into the shed and pulled shut the doors. "Cuts through alfalfa sod like butter."

Frank and Charlie, our draft horses that ordinarily pulled the plow, grazed quietly in the corner of the barnyard. They were growing fat and soft from lack of work.

That October, when we began digging potatoes, Pa said it was my turn to learn how to drive the tractor. Chain O' Lake School dismissed for two weeks of potato vacation so all the kids could help with the potato harvest. Some schools in the state had a spring vacation. Not Chain O' Lake. We had potato vacation in the fall when every man, boy, woman, and girl helped with the harvest so we could finish before the first killing frost ruined the crop.

Pa dropped the draw pin through the tongue of the steel-wheeled wagon, hooking it firmly to the tractor. Earlier he'd sawed several feet off the tongue because hooked to a tractor the tongue could be much shorter than when he used the team. He piled the wagon high with empty one-bushel wooden potato crates, and we drove out to the potato field. Pa hired Weston Coombes to help fork the potatoes out of the ground, and Weston and I sat on the wagon, our feet dangling over the side and kicking into the dirt when we wanted to.

My job was to pick up potatoes that Pa and Weston dug. They marched backwards, side by side across the field, each digging two rows of potatoes with six-tine barn forks. I followed along with a five-gallon pail, picking up the potatoes and dumping my full pail into one of the wooden boxes that we'd strung out across the twenty-acre field.

I still hadn't driven the tractor and wondered what Pa meant when he said today was the day I would learn. As noon approached, Pa stopped digging and suggested we load the filled boxes and haul them to the potato cellar near the chicken house.

"Come with me," Pa beckoned, as we walked to the homemade tractor parked under an oak tree that had turned a beautiful shade of reddish-brown. He hopped on the seat, pulled on the choke wire, pushed the starter button, and the engine caught the first time. Then he slid to the ground.

"Here," he said. "You drive. You're old enough to steer this thing while we pick up potato boxes."

"But how do I start moving?"

"Just push in the clutch, slip the shifting lever into dual low, put your other foot on the gas pedal, slowly let out the clutch, and push a little on the gas at the same time."

Sounded easy enough. I pushed in the clutch. I'd done this many times before, when I was play driving, so I knew how. I pulled on the lever and shifted into dual low. This I had also practiced before. Now I pushed on the gas pedal, and the engine roared a little and the machine began to vibrate. I pushed on the gas pedal some more.

"Not too much gas," Pa cautioned. He stood just back of me, on the tongue of the wagon. Slowly I let out the clutch, momentarily forgetting that my other foot continued to push on the gas pedal. With a mighty lurch, the tractor jumped forward, nearly toss-ing my father off his perch.

"Take your foot off the gas! Take your foot off the gas!" he yelled. I eased up on the gas pedal, and we moved slowly along the field. I was driving. By myself. For real. When we got to the end of the field, Pa showed me how to make a wide turn with the wagon, so the tractor's big rear tires wouldn't run into the front wheel of the wagon and break the wooden tongue. This I did without incident. I pushed in the clutch, shifted the lever into neutral, and jumped off the seat. A big smile spread across my face, and I felt a great sense of accomplishment. I heard people talk-ing about feeling like a man. This was surely what it was like. Being a man was a fine feeling.

"You're not done yet," Pa said. "Drive back across the field while Weston and I load these potato boxes on the wagon. Stop when I tell you to."

This time I did better with the clutch and gas pedal, and the tractor began moving along the soft potato ground. I stopped by the first several potato boxes while Weston and Pa promptly loaded them onto the wagon. Then I drove on. It was going well, exceedingly well. What was so complicated about driving a tractor, I wondered? Why all the fuss? There was nothing to it. A little steering to avoid running over the potato boxes and the potato plants not yet dug, a little thinking about how to let out the clutch and push down on the gas pedal at the same time, and listening to Pa say when I should stop and start. After two or three stops and starts, I had it down pat. I sat up straight on the tractor seat, hoping someone like maybe Jim Kolka would pass by on the road and see me driving the tractor. Kolkas didn't have a tractor—not a homemade one, not a factory-made one. Nothing. They depended for all their pulling on a pair of buckskin-colored draft horses, a rather tired pair that plodded along in a truly unspectacular way. What a great thing it would be if Jim or one of the other neighbor kids saw me driving this shiny new tractor, even if it wasn't factory built and didn't have the name John Deere or McCormick Deering or Fordson stamped on it. Model A Ford was good enough for me. Besides, everybody knew what a Model A Ford was. Several neighbors had Model A Ford cars and they swore by them, at them sometimes too, when they wouldn't start.

I approached the top of a rather steep hill. I stopped while Pa and Weston lifted several more potato boxes on the wagon, then I eased ahead, not quite sure how I should stop mid-hill. Stop I surely must for four or five filled potato boxes sat waiting half-way down the slope. Slowly I eased forward, the tractor gears holding the load back and making driving easier.

"Whoa!" Pa yelled. Much later, when we no longer had horses on the farm, he still yelled "Whoa!" when he meant stop.

I confidently pushed in the clutch and, rather than stop, the tractor began gaining speed.

"Push on the brake!" Pa yelled. I'd practiced this earlier but when the tractor was standing still. I pushed as hard as I could but nothing happened. The tractor with the partially loaded wagon of filled potato boxes moved even faster.

"Push on the brake!" Pa yelled again with some concern in his voice. I began staring at the brake pedal and my foot that somehow wasn't accomplishing the right thing. Glancing down was a major mistake.

"Look out for the potato boxes!" Pa yelled.

I looked up to see the right front tractor wheel hit the first wooden box dead center. I heard a sickening, splintering sound as the wood broke. I saw potatoes rolling down the hill. Then, before I could recover, I hit the next box, and the next, and the next, and somehow missed the last one on the hillside. At the bottom of the hill, I let out the clutch and killed the engine. I put my hands over my face, expecting the worst, when Pa caught up with the runaway rig.

"You hurt?" he asked, out of breath.

"Nah," I answered. "Smashed some boxes, didn't I?" The obvious was all I could think to say.

"Yup. Hop down and help Weston and me pick up the spilled potatoes and the kindling wood."

That's all he said. No punishment. No tongue lashing. Later, he showed me how to brace myself on the seat so I could get more leverage out of my right leg and push the brake far enough to stop the tractor. He also reminded me that had I gently let out the clutch, the tractor would also have stopped.

As I think about it now, I learned a lot more than a valuable driving lesson that day. I learned I shouldn't become confident too quickly when doing something new like driving a tractor. And I gained a new respect for Pa, too. By the end of the potato season, I was driving our shiny new tractor everywhere.

Barn Cats

Barn cats are a breed apart, animals that those who love ordinary cats could never understand. They come in all colors and sizes, ranging from black to white and nearly every color in between. On the home farm, we had between a half-dozen and fifteen cats—sometimes more. They lived in the barn and were never allowed in the house. They had but one purpose, controlling mice and other unwanted critters in and around the farm buildings. Most of the time they didn't have names. We merely referred to them by some physical characteristic—yellow cat, broken ear, limpy, spot, black nose.

Barn cats were not pets, but most of them were regulars at the milk dish in the barn. During the time we milked cows by hand, it was common to aim a stream of milk at an unwary feline and then watch it leap into the air as if it had been struck with a .22 bul-let. But cats are smart. After one or two of these milk-stream attacks, the cat learned to open its mouth and catch the stream of fresh milk. At succeeding milk-ings, the cat would do the same thing, much to the delight of city cousins visiting and watching these cow barn antics.

Other than a pan of fresh milk provided each morning and evening, we fed our cats nothing. Cats needed an incentive to catch mice. Pa said, a hungry cat makes a good mouser (a technical term for cats known to catch more than an average number of mice).

Kittens were born regularly, mostly somewhere in the barn's hayloft. My brothers and I kept mental notes on the cats at the milk dish and could usually tell, just by looking, which cats were expecting. We also noticed when a cat was missing at the cat dish for

a time or two; we'd then go scouting for the nest of baby kittens. Usually we'd find them, sometimes with their eyes still closed and totally dependent on their mother. Barn cats chose out-of-the-way places to give birth—behind a barn beam, near the hay chute (a partially covered hole in the floor through which hay was forked) or in a far corner of the haymow.

As much as we appreciated barn cats, none of us cared much for tomcats. Of course, the toms were necessary for a steady supply of kittens, but their negative characteristics far out-distanced anything positive about them. My personal dislike for tomcats began when I first became acquainted with the barn cat mating ritual. We called the female cats "she" cats, and when they were in heat they drew considerable attention, attracting tomcats from great distances.

One night I was awakened by the loudest, most blood-curdling yowling that I had ever heard. I told Pa the next morning that I was sure I heard a bobcat screaming during the night and that we ought to set a trap for it or the critter would take all our chickens for sure.

"Wasn't no bobcat you heard, only a couple of cats breedin'," Pa said with a broad grin on his face.

I had seen bulls breed cows, even helped with the process by herding the cow while Pa handled the bull. I had seen roosters breeding hens and boar pigs breeding sows, and for none of this coming together was there such a sound as these two barn cats had made. I didn't know what to make of it, but decided this was a topic better discussed behind the outhouse at school with the older boys than with Pa, so I let the matter drop. Of course, I knew that in a few weeks we could expect some new kittens, so I tucked that bit of information into my head and went about doing my chores.

Nature knows what it is doing. Right on schedule the kittens were born. My brothers and I found the six little ones in a nest the mother cat had made in the haymow of the old barn. Every day we crawled up into the mow and played a little with the kittens. We figured we could tame this litter some and they wouldn't be so wild when they finally made their way downstairs and crowded up to the milk dish with the other barn cats. But this was not to happen.

One late afternoon, when my brothers and I climbed the ladder to the haymow, we found a dead kitten at the top of the stairs, its head nearly severed and blood spilled all over the hay. A bit farther on we found another dead kitten that had met a similar fate and more blood.

I knew immediately what had happened. The tomcat had returned and killed the kittens. Pa told us that this happened often. With the kittens dead, the mother would come back in heat. I never expected such a heinous act would occur in our barn, but there were the dead kittens—gruesome evidence of a tom-cat's savage urges.

I squinted my eyes for a better look at the carnage and, much to my surprise, caught the outline of a huge cat lying on a pile of hay toward the back of the mow. I whispered to my brothers, "It's the tomcat that killed the kittens." We had seen the tom at the milk dish regularly over the past couple of years. Who would have thought that this rather docile-looking tomcat was actually a kitten killer? My mind was reeling. What could we do to save the remaining kittens? Some must still be living or the tomcat wouldn't be hanging around.

I said to my brothers, "Keep an eye on that tom while I fetch some equipment."

I had made up my mind that we were going to catch this killer tomcat and punish him for his deeds. I hadn't yet decided what the punishment ought to be. Had he been an unknown cat, the decision would have been easy. Kill him. But we needed to think of something less than killing for punishment. After all, this old tom had probably caught more mice and rats than we could ever have imagined. Such good deeds should be worth something. Still, as I climbed down the ladder from the haymow, I was angry enough to want to fetch my .22 rifle from the gun closet in the kitchen and shoot the killer in the head.

Instead, I found several burlap bags in the granary and ran back to the barn with them hoping that the tom had not leaped by my brothers and escaped.

"He still here?" I whispered when I crawled back up the ladder to the haymow.

"Yup. Still here," Murf said. "Geeze, he's big. Looks twice as big as a she cat."

The tom lay crouched on the hay, his eyes exuding

hatred. Pa told us to never mess with a cornered tom-cat as they can claw, bite, and do all sorts of damage to a person. This one looked like he was ready to attack at any minute.

"Whatta you gonna do with the gunny bags?" Duck whispered.

"Throw 'em over the tomcat," I said with more confidence in my voice than I was feeling at that moment.

"Here. Each of you guys take one of the bags, and we'll sneak up on the cat and grab him. And remember, no matter what happens, don't let go."

In the near dark of the barn's upstairs—there were no windows—we moved like three soldiers on combat patrol with the enemy in view. We had heard relatives who had returned from World War II talk about combat patrols, and this surely seemed like what they described. Except the enemy was a big, old, mean tomcat that lay quietly, sprawled out on a pile of hay and ready to spring.

The yellow tom growled a deep throaty snarl.

"You sure we should do this?" Murf said quietly. "He's really big and mean looking."

"Nothin' to it," I said. I hoped I sounded more confident than I felt. "Just remember. Don't let go. When I say 'now', we'll each jump on the cat with our gunny bags."

Each of us grabbed the corners of the bags and eased forward as slowly as possible so as not to spook the cat. Duck stepped full face into a massive cobweb. He started spitting and making the most awful face.

"Keep your eyes on the cat," I whispered. I knew that cobwebs did not distract a combat soldier, even when the dusty things got in his mouth.

"Ready?" I whispered. Each of us lifted up our gunny bag. I noticed that Murf's bag had a big hole in it, but this was no time to point out the inadequacy of his combat equipment.

"Now!" I yelled. The three of us jumped on the tomcat at the same time.

The tom immediately began growling and howling and clawing. I hadn't counted on his teeth either. As he thrashed and clawed, he bit whatever was handy. Thankfully, his strong rat-killing jaws came down on hunks of burlap.

"Don't let go!" I yelled. "We got him! We got

him!" I probably sounded a lot more sure of the capture than was the reality of the situation. At the moment the cat was winning the battle. I could see by the expressions on my brothers' faces that maybe we should call a truce and turn the tom lose.

"Hold on!" I yelled. "Hold on! He'll tire soon." But who would tire first, three little boys or one very mad tomcat?

Soon, to my relief, the thrashing and caterwauling subsided and it was quiet once more in the haymow above the barn.

"Don't ease up," I warned. "Cat might get a second wind."

"Maybe we killed him," Murf said.

"Doubt that," I said. "Takes more than a little tussle with gunny bags to kill a tomcat, especially an old mean one like this."

"Now here's what we're gonna do," I said. "We're gonna shove this old tom into one of these gunny bags and tie the top." I'd remembered to stuff a length of binding twine in my back pocket when I'd gone for the burlap bags.

"Murf, you hold on tight. I'll hold on tight. And Duck, you let go and hold open the top of your bag and we'll stuff the cat in there and tie it shut."

And that's what we did. The old tom was surely not dead, but we'd knocked some of the fight out of him, at least for the moment. I quickly tied shut the top of the bag, and we started down the stairway to the stable below.

The tom kicked a little and growled some, but nothing like when we first dropped the gunny bags over him a few minutes earlier.

"What're we gonna do now?" Duck asked.

"We're gonna castrate him. When we're done, this tomcat won't kill anymore little kittens."

"How we gonna do that?" Murf wondered.

"Same way Pa castrates little pigs," I answered. One of my jobs for the last few years was to hold the little pigs while Pa castrated them. I had watched closely and I figured I knew just how to do it.

"You guys watch the cat while I find the castrating knife and some disinfectant," I said.

I found Pa's straight-edge razor that he used for castrating, ran it over the razor strap to put a fine edge on it (this is what Pa always did), and, for disinfectant, dumped some Lysol into a coffee can half-full of water.

"We're ready," I said. "Except we need one of Pa's rubber boots to hold the cat." Duck ran to the woodshed for it. Pa once said that if you ever wanted to castrate a tomcat you should push his head into a boot. I doubt he ever thought we'd try the procedure, but he had given us powerful information nonetheless.

The equipment was in place. We'd set up our operating room out back of the granary, in the shadow of the corncrib and just beyond the straw stack. We didn't want Pa to stumble onto our little project. We'd have to go into some detail to explain what we were doing and why we were doing it, and none of us wanted to be bothered with all this explaining when we were ready to change a tomcat's mind about killing little kittens.

I untied the bag, and we eased the tomcat into the boot. He growled and snarled a couple of times and kicked some, but the shift from gunny bag to knee-high rubber boot came off without a hitch.

"Murf, you keep a good grip on the boot, and hold on no matter what. We don't want this old tom to get away now."

"I will," Murf said as he grabbed the boot.

"Duck, I want you to hold his back legs apart."

"I will," Duck said.

I swished the razor around in the Lysol water and washed my fingers. (Pa always did this when we castrated pigs. "Never lost a pig from infection," he said.)

"Everybody ready?" I asked.

"Yup," said Murf, as he tightened his grip on the boot.

"Yup," said Duck, as he increased his hold on the cat's back legs.

I felt around the cat's testicles a little, to make sure I knew exactly where I wanted to cut. (Pa always felt a pig's testicles before he made the first incision.) Then I rubbed a little Lysol on the place where I figured I should make a slit.

The moment the razor cut the skin the tom let out such a yowl that I was sure Pa would hear, maybe even the neighbors who lived a mile away would hear. I'd never heard such a cry. It was even louder than when I'd heard the she cat and the tom going to it that night several weeks ago.

At the moment the tom began yowling, he sent a stream of urine against Duck's overalls, about the place where he'd carry a pocket watch if he had one. And such a powerful stream it was and it didn't stop either. I stopped cutting for an instant to watch. When Duck realized what was happening, he stepped aside a little and the urine stream shot up into the air. Later, as we recalled the incident, all three of us agreed that the tom had shot a stream of urine near as high as the straw stack. That is some accomplishment, for man or beast.

We were all so busy watching this high-pressured stream that we failed to notice that the tom was biting through the boot and beginning to make Murf's job difficult.

I continued cutting, successfully removing the first testicle, and ready to start with the second.

"Cat bit me. Cat bit me!" Murf yelled as he dropped the boot. With the boot on the ground, the tom shot out of it like he had been propelled by a charge of gunpowder. The last glimpse we had of him was when he cleared the fence by the woods and disappeared into the underbrush.

"Doubt he'll kill any kittens for a while," I said.

"Bet he'll die," Duck offered.

"Don't care if he does," Murf said, staring at the bite marks on his finger.

"Swish your finger around in the Lysol water," I suggested. "Make sure you don't get an infection." Murf did that before we gathered up our operating equipment and closed down the operating room.

"What'll Pa say?" Duck asked.

"We won't tell him," I suggested.

A few days later the old yellow tom showed up at the milk dish in the barn.

"What's the matter with that old tom?" Pa asked. "He's walking awful stiff."

"Cow must have kicked him," I said.

"Doubt that," Pa said, looking at me with a grin. He didn't ask anymore questions and we didn't offer anymore answers.

We never caught that yellow tom killing any more kittens. But about a year later, I was awakened one night by cat yowls. I looked out the window, and in the deep night shadows, I spotted the old yellow tom with a she cat.

Music Education

One of the few radio programs that came in clearly on our battery radio was the WLS Barn Dance from Chicago. It was broadcast every Saturday night and included an assortment of performers: Lulu Bell and Scotty, Red Blanchard, the Hoosier Hot Shots, and many more. They played music—beautiful music— and sang songs in a way that I didn't think possible. The barn dance singers set my standard for good singing: Whenever I listened to somebody sing, whether at church, school, or the county fair, I always compared them to the Barn Dance folks, who I knew were the best singers anywhere in the world.

How I wished that I could sing and play like those performers. And one day, opportunity arrived.

Before my brothers and I were old enough to help with the heavy fieldwork, Pa employed a hired man each spring to work through the planting, growing, and harvesting season. I don't remember that he ever hired the same fellow two years in a row, so each year we had a new experience. The hired man lived with us as a member of the family. He ate with us and had his own bedroom upstairs in the house.

The summer I was eleven, Pa hired Henry Lackelt. Henry, a tall, slim man in his early twenties, loved country music. When he showed up at our farm looking for work, he carried a jacket over his arm, an old, ragged-looking suitcase, and a shiny guitar. The guitar caught my attention because outside of seeing guitar players at the county fair, this was the first time I had seen a guitar up close. It was a beautiful instrument, shiny reddish-brown with a long neck and six black adjusting knobs, three on each side. And I immediately was reminded of the WLS Barn Dance.

Henry became my summer friend the minute he

73

said, "Wanna hole my gee-tar?"

He had a way of speaking that was different from folks in our community. He let his words float out there, one at a time, nice and easy, with a lot of room between each of them. Pa told me Henry had come from the south and that people talked different down there.

"Can I?" I replied.

"Don drop hit," Henry said, smiling.

I immediately fell in love with Henry's guitar and hoped that some day I might have one just like it. Nearly every evening, when the chores were finished, Henry took up the instrument, ran his finger across the strings, and then began playing and singing. Such beautiful sounds. Almost as good as the Barn Dance. The music was sweet and clear. He crossed his legs, strummed the strings, and sang "That Silver-Haired Daddy of Mine," "Red River Valley," "Home on the Range," and many other songs.

I watched in amazement, marveling at how such sweet music could come from a wooden instrument with six strings and a hole in it.

"How do you do that?" I asked.

"Nothin' to hit," Henry said. The way he talked made his singing more interesting. He sounded a lot like those professional singers I heard on the radio.

The more I listened to Henry sing and play his guitar, the more I knew I wanted to learn how. By the time that fall rolled around and it was time for Henry to leave, I dreaded not having his guitar to entertain us nearly every evening. But then Henry did the most wonderful thing. The day before he left, he asked, "Jerry, you wanna buy this old gee-tar? Hain't hardly worth carrin' it along with me anyway."

I was afraid to ask how much he wanted because all the money I had saved was three dollars and twenty-seven cents, which I had planned to use mostly for Christmas presents.

"Whad' ya think a two bucks?" Henry asked.

"I'll take it," I said, without even asking Pa what he thought about the deal. Henry handed me a little, stained, dog-eared book filled with music and words for twenty-five different songs that could be played on the guitar.

"See this eer book? Well, all you do is follow these lil diagreems. That tells you war to put yer fingers on the strings."

I looked, and sure enough there were instructions on how to play the G chord and the D chord or whatever the song required. Above the words were the designated chords.

The day after Henry left, I took out my new guitar and, with the dog-eared book on my lap, began strumming. Immediately I discovered that playing a guitar was a lot harder than it looked. I kept trying until Ma said I should either quit or I should take some music lessons because the sound coming out of the guitar was nothing like what came out of it when Henry played. She told me she would talk to Mrs. Darling in town about giving me lessons—fifty cents an hour she charged. Mrs. Darling mostly gave piano lessons but said she knew something about guitar. Ma said she'd use some of her egg money to pay for the teaching because she knew how much I wanted to learn how to play.

When Mrs. Darling, an older, gray-haired woman, saw my guitar for the first time she gave a little gasp.

"Where'd you get this?" she asked, not able to hide her look of surprise. I suspect she saw all the scratches and nicks and didn't really see the beauty of the instrument or appreciate the wonderful sounds that came from it.

"Bought it from our hired man. Paid him two dollars," I answered. Mrs. Darling covered her mouth with her hand, but I could tell that she was smiling. At the time, I figured she thought I had gotten a pretty good deal, because the cheapest guitar you could buy from the Sears catalog was up to fifteen or twenty dollars and that was before shipping charges.

"Well, let's see if we can tune it," she said as she led me into the living room and sat me down in a straight-backed chair near her piano. The living room was dark with heavy curtains on the windows and flowered wallpaper that was barely visible.

Alternately she hit a piano key and then plucked a string on the guitar. This process she repeated again and again until I thought she surely was wearing out the instrument by plucking on the strings and screwing the black knobs. Henry never went to all this trouble before he played, but then we didn't have a piano at home so he couldn't.

"That's about the best I can do," she finally said. "Guitar's seen better days. Are you ready?"

"I am," I replied. I didn't know what I should be ready for, but it seemed the right thing to say.

"Watch what I do," she said as she cradled the guitar on her expansive lap and carefully plucked out some music. The long, skinny fingers of her left hand slid effortlessly along the strings, stopping here and there. Music came from the guitar but not the same wonderful country music that Henry played.

"There are two ways to play this instrument," she said. Her words came out short and sharp, in direct contrast with Henry's slow and easy way with words.

"You can play chords or you can play notes. Playing chords isn't really playing though, so we're going to learn notes," she said as she wiped back some hair that seemed to slip over her right eye from time to time.

This was starting to sound a lot more complicated than I bargained for, but I knew my mother was paying fifty cents an hour of her hard-earned egg money so I tried to pay attention. All I wanted to do was play my guitar like Henry did, not learn a bunch of notes.

Mrs. Darling went on, "Just remember F-A-C-E. Those are the notes on the staff between the lines." She showed me a picture with a lot of lines on it and some notes scattered here and there.

"Oh, don't forget that this is called a staff," she said pointing out the lines on the page. Now I was puzzled. I knew about a staff, and it was nothing like this at all. A staff was a heavy piece of pipe with a hook on the end that Pa snapped onto our bull's ring when he led him outside the barn to breed a cow. Now Mrs. Darling was calling these lines on a page a staff. I didn't say anything. I knew that sometimes it was best to remain quiet when you had more information than your teacher.

"Next, remember the letters E-G-B-D-F. They are the notes on the lines. You can remember them by thinking 'Every good boy does fine.' The notes go from A to G."

Right here I began to suspect that music was shortchanging itself by stopping with the letter G. After all, there is a considerable number of letters from H to Z, and the music people didn't use any of them. On the other hand, I could see that there was scarcely enough room on the note page for those from A to G; if you added the rest, the whole thing would be so cluttered you couldn't make head nor tail of it.

What it came down to, as I heard Mrs. Darling try to explain all this to me, was I didn't want anything to do with notes, no matter how many there were. I just wanted to learn how to play my guitar.

"Why do I have to learn all these notes?" I innocently asked. "Show me how to play my guitar so I can sing songs like they do on the WLS Barn Dance in Chicago."

"The what?" Mrs. Darling said.

"The Barn Dance in Chicago, the one that comes over the radio."

"I'm afraid I've never heard of that radio program," Mrs. Darling said.

Now I was confused. How could anyone who taught music, especially guitar, not know about the Barn Dance in Chicago. If you didn't listen to the Barn Dance how could you ever know if your playing and singing were any good? You needed to listen to the best so you could make a comparison.

Mrs. Darling was anxious to get away from talking about high-quality singers and exemplary guitar playing.

"First things first," she said. "You learn how to read music and then you learn how to play your guitar."

By this time, my first hour of music lessons was over and I sat on the front steps of Mrs. Darling's house waiting for Pa to pick me up so I could get home in time to help with the chores.

"How'd it go?" Pa said. He could see my hound-dog look, as he called someone's appearance when they weren't happy.

"She wants me to learn how to read music," I replied.

"Thought you were gonna learn how to play Henry's old guitar."

"That's what I want. But Mrs. Darling has other ideas."

"Maybe it will go better next time," Pa said. "First time doin' anything is often a problem." Neither of us spoke the rest of the ride home.

"How'd it go?" Ma asked when we came into the

house. I put down my guitar, not knowing quite how to answer. Music lessons were clearly not what I had expected.

"Fine," I said, in a quiet voice. I hoped that Pa was right and that I'd learn more about playing my guitar next week. Music lessons were scheduled for an hour every Wednesday night.

The next week it was the same and the week after that, too. Mrs. Darling had reading music on her mind, and all I wanted to do was learn how to play my guitar like our hired man, Henry, had done.

When Pa picked me up after the third music lesson, I told him about how Mrs. Darling was trying to teach me a bunch of stuff I didn't want to learn.

"It's like some foreign language," I said. "All those squiggly lines splashed on a piece of paper with straight lines all over it. Besides, I'm not learning much about playing my guitar."

"No sense going back to Mrs. Darling if you ain't learnin' how to play that thing," Pa said, agreeing with me.

That night, after I had gone off to bed, I heard some loud talking in the kitchen. Ma and Pa must have been talking about my guitar and the music lessons. I wondered how the discussion came out. The next morning I learned.

"No more music lessons," Pa said. "Costs too much and you're not learnin' how to play."

That was the end of my formal music training. I continued strumming away on the guitar, following Henry's book. I even learned how to tune the strings with a tuning pipe that someone gave me. Then one day, in the midst of playing "Red River Valley," the guitar's bridge, the part that holds the strings in place, pulled loose from its base and I couldn't replace it.

I never did learn to play a guitar. But I still can hear Henry Lackelt strumming "Red River Valley," his legs crossed and the words floating on the cool night air. I know that if only I had the right teacher, I could play it, too.

Frank, Pinky, and Harry

You could hear the sound of music a half-mile away, especially on a hot summer day when there was no wind and dust lifted from the country road and hung in the air like a dirty blanket. The music ranged from polkas and waltzes and schottisches to more haunting tunes that reminded the musician and his wife of the Old Country, of Czechoslovakia.

Almost every Sunday afternoon in summer, Frank Kolka took out his concertina (a squeezebox, some of the neighbors called it), sat on a chair, and played beautiful music. He played for his family—Mrs. Kolka had been born in Czechoslovakia—and for any neighbors who might be driving by. And he played for himself, as he leaned back in his chair, worked the fifty-one buttons on the instrument, and let the music flow. Each button played a different note on the push and the pull.

While my brothers and I attended Chain O' Lake School, we got to know the Kolka boys, Jim and Dave, very well. They lived only a mile from our farm, straight to the west as the crow flies and a little farther by road because the road made a few twists and turns and went up and down a couple of hills along the way. Jim was half a year younger than I was; his brother was a couple of years younger. They were the closest kids to our farm, and Sundays were a good time to visit them.

I remember the first time my brothers and I heard the music when we were walking along the road to their farm on a Sunday afternoon. It sounded like a radio playing in the distance and I said that to my brothers, who also could hear the sound.

"But it can't be a radio," I said. "Plays only music, and it's so clear—no static." Nobody could listen to a radio in our neighborhood without picking up static; the radio stations were just too far away. The exception was at night, especially a winter night. Then some of the stations came in strong and clear, especially WGN and WLS out of Chicago.

When we reached the top of the hill, from which we could see the Kolkas' farmhouse in the distance, the music became even clearer. As we walked along, we could see Frank on the porch, squeezing away on something from which beautiful music came. His long fingers bounced around the keyboard. A smile spread across his tanned, weathered face. After greeting Jim and Dave, I pointed to the instrument and asked what it was called.

"It's a Pearl Queen concertina," Frank Kolka answered. "Any particular tune you wanna hear?"

I said I didn't know any songs for him to play. I didn't know much about music. The only songs I was familiar with were "Red River Valley" and "She'll Be Coming 'Round the Mountain," tunes I had heard on the WLS Barn Dance from Chicago on Saturday night. But I didn't want to mention those songs because he seemed to be playing a different kind of music.

Frank Kolka began playing again, pushing and pulling on this rather unusual instrument with buttons on each side and a leather-like material in the middle that folded and unfolded when he pushed and pulled on it. Soon all of us were tapping our feet to the music, allowing it to become a part of us. This was the first time I had heard polka music and old-time waltzes, as some people called them. Outside of the WLS program, the only music I had listened to was church organ music and that was about as exciting as walking in deep mud. Of course, there was piano music at school, which was sometimes fun but often not.

Frank Kolka's music was fun. It was exciting. It had a beat. It was something you wanted to listen to. And it had lots of variation too, going from fast to slow, from quiet to raucous, from happy to sad. Frank played "Red Wing," "The Red Handkerchief Waltz," and "Springtime in the Rockies." He played "The Barbara Polka" (Mrs. Kolka's name was Barbara) and "The Pond Lily Waltz." And he mixed in Czech tunes. Tunes from the Old Country. Tunes that evoked memories.

When we returned home that afternoon, I told Pa

about Frank and his concertina.

"Yup. Frank can make that squeezebox talk," Pa said. "Sometime I gotta take you someplace where Harry is playing his fiddle."

Pa then told me about Harry Banks, whom I knew because he lived right across the road from Kolkas' farm. I knew that Harry Banks, an Englishman, tall and thin, was a farmer and part of the threshing crew that came to our farm, but I hadn't heard about his fiddle playing.

"Few people play the fiddle like Harry," Pa said.

"How does he do it?" I asked.

"Harry caught his hand in a hay mower a few years ago. It cut off a finger on his left hand."

It was not an unusual accident. Many of the farmers I knew had parts of fingers missing, lots of scars from being cut, and sometimes entire hands and even arms missing because of farm accidents.

"You gotta give it to Harry," Pa said, "He doesn't let a missing finger on his left hand stop his fiddle playing. He taught himself to play with three fingers."

While I was pondering how someone could play fiddle with only three fingers, Pa brought up another neighbor who played an instrument.

"Bet you don't know that Pinky Eserhut plays the banjo." Pa said.

I didn't know much about Pinky Eserhut. I didn't even know how he got his first name, which seemed a bit strange, even in our rural community where there were many unusual names. Pa explained that Pinky's hair was a kind of reddish color, which was probably the reason for his name. His real first name was Alvin.

I didn't know anything about banjos and what kind of music they made. Pa didn't play an instrument and didn't know much about music, but he tried to explain that a banjo was something like a guitar and had strings, a bigger end, and a longer neck that was attached to it.

He said that the bigger end was like a little drum with a piece of leather stretched across it. When you strummed the strings the sound was like a cross between a guitar and a drum.

Pa went on to tell me that from time to time Frank, Pinky, and Harry came together as a band and played for wedding dances, birthday parties, or any other occasion for which a group of people gathered to have some fun.

As good fortune would have it, Bill and Lorraine Miller were celebrating their wedding anniversary the following Saturday night, and we were all invited— Ma, Pa, my twin brothers and me. This would give me a chance to see the local band perform, and my first chance to see people dancing to polka and old-time waltz music.

By the time we arrived at the Chain O' Lake School, somebody had already moved all the desks to the side and the three musicians were up in front, tuning their instruments. At least that's what Ma said when I asked her what they were doing.

Cars were pulling up in the school yard, the women were gathering inside, and the men were standing around the front steps, smoking their pipes and sharing stories about their corn and cows and the price of potatoes.

My twin brothers, who were nearly four years younger than I was, trailed behind Ma inside the schoolhouse. I stayed outside with Pa. But we weren't out there long before the band began playing the first number. I asked Pa what it was and he said he thought it was "The Beer Barrel Polka." But since he didn't dance much he said I should ask Bill Miller. Bill was too busy celebrating his anniversary to answer such a question, so I didn't ask. I just found myself a seat next to the water cooler and watched with considerable amazement.

The people here were folks I knew, our neighbors in the Chain O' Lake community, but I had never seen them dance. Couples were swinging around the floor, hopping ever so often like jackrabbits and stamping their feet like I thought the floor might break. Polka dancing looked like hard work, especially on a warm summer evening. Nobody seemed bothered by the temperature, though; they were all grinning from ear to ear as they hopped around the floor in time with the music. Even Mrs. York was out there dancing with her husband, Guy, and she was smiling. I didn't remember that I'd ever seen her smile, but she was this evening. Something about polka music, I decided, seemed to lift worries off people's backs. I knew there was plenty to worry about. It hadn't rained much all summer, the hay was short, the corn plants could scarcely keep ahead of the weeds, and the oat crop, especially on the hilly farms, was mighty slim. No matter. Everybody was dancing the polka.

I focused my attention on the band, trying to figure out how such wonderful music could come from three farmers. Frank Kolka sat in the middle of the threesome, his concertina on his lap. Harry Banks, the three-fingered fiddler, stood to his right, and Pinky Eserhut, all decked out in a red shirt and a new pair of bib overalls, sat on the other side of Frank. There wasn't a scrap of printed music anywhere. All three of them played by ear-picking up tunes as they heard them. And they were having fun making music, such beautiful music as I had never heard before.

They played three polkas in a row, and then stopped to check with each other about what to play next. Looking around the room, I thought that some of the dancers were gonna keel over either from becoming overheated or from over exertion. I hadn't seen so much sweat since the last time we threshed.

The dancers had scarcely moved from the center of the floor when the band slipped into an old-time waltz. Now, an old-time waltz isn't all that much slower than a polka, but there is less hopping and no foot pounding. I suspect some city visitor might say the waltz is a more civilized kind of dance than the polka. But there is surely nothing uncivilized about the polka, once you know something about it and appreciate the fine music that's necessary for dancing it.

As the evening moved on, the music became sweeter and finer, at least that's how it sounded to me. And you could almost feel people's problems lift from their shoulders. You could see the transformation, too, in people's faces, in their laughter, and in the lightness of their steps.

Before the evening was over, I found myself liking the music from this little three-piece band even better than the WLS Barn Dance from Chicago. Maybe it was because I could see the three musicians as well as hear them. Maybe it was because there weren't any breaks to advertise cow feed or Keystone barb wire. Maybe because Frank, Pinky, and Harry taught me that music is good for more things than tapping your toes. On this one night, people put their problems aside and experienced the joy of living, a feeling that was mighty scarce in our community during bad years.

Deer Hunting

It was commonly understood in our neighborhood that no boy became a man until he'd gone deer hunting. Squirrel and rabbit hunting didn't count. Most boys had rifles and were hunting small game by the time they were ten years old, sometimes even younger. But state law said that you had to be twelve years old to hunt deer.

With my twelfth birthday in July, I could hardly wait until the third Saturday in November, when deer season opened. For my birthday, my folks gave me a fine new hunting knife with a six-inch blade, a leather handle, and a shiny leather case that you fastened to your belt. Pa showed me how to sharpen it so you could cut paper and even shave the hair off your arm.

Each fall, Pa and Bill Miller, a few years younger than Pa and our nearest neighbor to the south, drove some twenty-five miles west of our farm to hunt deer during the November season. Most of the time they came back with at least one buck tied to the fender of Pa's '36 Plymouth. We had fresh venison for several weeks.

Pa hunted deer with a 30-30 Savage rifle; Bill Miller used a 30-30 Marlin. These were powerful rifles compared to the .22 that we used to hunt squirrels and rabbits. These 30-30s were designed to kill large animals, such as a deer, quickly and humanely. But Pa said that for my first year deer hunting I'd have to use his old 12-gauge double-barrel shotgun with slugs. Ordinarily, the shotgun shot lead pellets and was used for hunting pheasants, grouse, ducks, and Canada geese. For deer hunting, the law required the use of solid lead bullets called slugs. A 12-gauge lead slug was as big as the end of your thumb clear up to the first joint and would knock a deer down as fast as a 30-30 bullet. The problem was accuracy. Shotguns were made for shooting shot, not slugs. Some deer hunters, mostly those who carried deer rifles, offered that shooting a shotgun at a deer was akin to using a sling shot. Both had about the same accuracy.

I'd heard all the stories about shotguns that shot around corners and were off as much as six feet from where you aimed. Shotguns don't have rear sights for aiming, just a little metal bead on the end of the barrel. So you didn't aim a shotgun, you pointed it. With fine shot it didn't matter. If you came close to your target, usually a few lead pellets would connect and do the job. But with lead slugs, you either hit something or you didn't.

I'd used some of my savings to buy two boxes of slugs—twelve bullets, which I figured should last for at least two years. Ideally, I should have taken that old blunderbuss of a gun out to the far gully and fired at some tin cans to see how crooked it shot. But with the price of 12-gauge slugs, I figured I'd take my chances and not waste any bullets shooting at cans. Sure as could be, just when I needed another bullet to finish

off a giant ten-point buck, I wouldn't have one, and I'd wished I hadn't wasted slugs target practicing.

Saturday, November 15, finally rolled around. Pa and I got up at four to milk the cows and do the barn chores. Quickly we ate breakfast, grabbed up our hunting gear, stopped for Bill Miller, and turned on County A for the trip west. Conversation focused on buck deer shot and buck deer missed, on buck deer seen and buck deer heard, when, where and under what circumstances. I'd listened to all the stories before, told around the kitchen table again and again, whenever Pa and Bill got together. Each time in the telling, they were slightly more exaggerated than the previous time.

I had been to the hunting area before, near a place called the Mound, a high rise of ground that stuck up above country that was otherwise quite flat. Pa always drove past the place where he was born, in 1899, and past the site of the log schoolhouse that he had attended. Now, no buildings could be found at either site. A mile or so from his birthplace, we parked the Plymouth in an open field, alongside a woods.

"This is the place," Pa said. "Just beyond those jack pines is where I missed that big one last year."

The three of us spread out in the woods, maybe a hundred yards or so apart, close enough so we could glimpse each other once in a while. We walked for ten minutes or so, then stood for maybe fifteen minutes, and then walked some more. The woods smelled sweet and clean, with a pungency that comes from dead grass and fallen leaves. The sky was brilliant blue, not a cloud. And not a sound either, except once in mid-morning when a late flock of Canada geese flew over, their complaining honks settling over the woods like a giant blanket. Then it was quiet again.

Each step was the ultimate in expectancy. I walked with one finger on the outside of the trigger guard, my thumb ready to pull back the hammer in preparation for shooting. I walked through hazel brush and black raspberry bushes that tore at my clothing and scratched my hands. I walked around huge old white pine trees that had been blown over in a summer windstorm. I kept an eagle eye out for Bill, a long-legged fellow with an easy stroll, who walked on one side of me, and Pa, who walked on the other. I thought about getting lost and I surely didn't want to. Not here in this wild country with no farmers or few other inhabitants. Not here when you sometimes could walk four miles or more before coming to a road, which might only be a logging trail. If I got lost, it would spoil the hunt, for Pa would have to waste valuable hunting time searching for me.

We alternately walked and stood all that morning, and none of us saw a deer, not even a doe. Nothing. I did see a few red squirrels and a couple of ruffed grouse that exploded in front of me, surprising me so that I raised up the old double-barrel thinking it might be a deer. But there were no deer.

"Let's eat our dinner," Pa said. "This afternoon, we'll drive over to that high ground beyond the river." He was referring to the Roche-a-Cri River, which ran through the area.

After a quick meal of cold sandwiches and a couple of cookies, we drove across the wooden bridge spanning the Roche-a-Cri, up the rather steep grade on the other side, and on for another quarter mile or so.

"Let's hope our luck is better on this side of the

river," Pa said.

"Can't get any worse," Bill offered, checking his 30-30 to make sure it was ready.

"Let's do it a little different this time," Pa suggested. "Jerold and I will make a little drive through these woods. Bill, you go down to the crossroad and watch what comes out. If there's anything in there, we'll send it your way. We'll hoot once in a while so you know where we are."

Here the woods were a little less brushy than where we had been in the morning; we could spread out and still glimpse each other well. By yelping like a dog or making other loud noises such as "Arr-RUP, Arr-RUP," we could hear each other and didn't always have to depend on sight.

This was my first deer drive. I quickly learned that driving deer is an art, especially the yelling part, and it took some time to learn how to do it well. You perfected a particular call that was yours and yours alone so your hunting partners always knew where you were by how you yelled. And you needed to yell loudly enough so that on a clear, quiet day you could be heard for at least a mile. Most deer drives were at least that long.

I practiced a couple of yells, including yapping like a dog, but couldn't generate enough volume. Finally, after walking a hundred yards or so, I settled on a version of "Arr-RUP, Arr-RUP" that worked to my satisfaction. Of course, I wouldn't know for sure how it worked until I had a chance to check with Bill after the drive and find out if he heard me; I knew Pa could because he was much closer.

The main purpose of the noise was to scare the deer out of the woods so the hunter stationed at the edge could have a clear shot. I was concentrating on my yell, varying the volume a little and trying to holler and walk at the same time, without running out of breath. I had just let out what I figured was my best call yet, a powerful "Arr-RUPP" that seemed to echo back at me, when I glimpsed out of the corner of my eye a movement to the right, under some oak trees. I froze and glanced in that direction. At first I didn't see anything, just the floor of brown fallen leaves and the grayish black trunks of oak trees. Then I caught the movement again. Rabbit was my first thought, maybe a jackrabbit, because what I saw were brown ears flicking back and forth, two pair of them.

I followed the ears down to the heads. My gosh almighty, here were deer, two of them, lying down in the leaves, their ears flopping back and forth, trying to pick up that strange sound they'd earlier heard. My heart began pounding, my finger found the trigger guard, and my thumb eased back the hammer. Was one of them a buck? That was the question. The one in front was surely a doe, because I could see no horns, just a pair of long brown ears. I strained my eyes to see the other head. What I had earlier thought was a little dead branch turned out to be deer horns, big deer horns. Now my heart really began to pound, so loudly I was sure the deer could hear it thumping.

The buck was resting behind the doe with only its head and neck visible. I raised up the double-barrel gun, slowly because I knew deer spook easily. The biggest problem was that they were lying down. How

was I supposed to shoot a deer that was still on its bed? Pa never said anything about shooting deer lying down. So I had no information about how to shoot.

He'd told me how to shoot a standing deer. "Aim just behind the shoulder," he said. "Bullet will pass through the lungs, probably hit the heart, and the deer will die within minutes—never know what hit it. It's humane, just like slaughtering a pig."

I couldn't see a shoulder. Just horns and ears, and a sliver of the buck's neck. Not much of a target. I remember Pa saying how he'd shot a deer once in the neck and it dropped in its tracks, kicked once or twice, and died.

I pulled back the hammer and lifted the double-barrel to my shoulder, carefully trying to hold the front bead sight on the buck's neck. The barrel jumped up and down, shaking as my heart pounded. I took a deep breath, held it, pointed at the buck's neck, and pulled the trigger.

"Kaboom!" the double-barrel gun roared. I stumbled back a couple of steps. The 12-gauge kicked like someone had hit me in the shoulder with a sledge hammer. My ears were ringing, my hands were shaking, and through the gun smoke I tried to see if my trophy lay there in the leaves.

Finally, I saw the two deer. They had jumped up and were standing together looking at me, flicking their ears back and forth. Neither had been touched. Then their long white tails flew up and they bounded off, disappearing among the trees.

My feeling of great excitement and anticipation quickly turned to disappointment and disgust. How could I have missed a buck deer when it was lying down and not that far away either, clearly within the range of the double-barrel shotgun? I wanted to sit down in the leaves and cry, I felt so bad. Here was my first great opportunity to bag a buck deer and a big one, too, and I muffed it. Missed clear and simple. What would I say to Pa and Bill? That I saw a buck deer resting in the leaves and I missed? How could I explain what happened without evoking roaring laughter from my hunting partners?

I knew that I must keep walking and yelling, or Pa would think I had killed a deer and would walk over to help me field dress it. Right now I didn't want to face Pa, or anyone else for that matter. So I went back to yelling and walking, hoping that maybe I'd run onto another sleeping buck and get a second chance or, perhaps even better, see one standing broadside from me so I could aim behind the shoulder and have better luck.

Later, when I stumbled onto the crossroad and found Bill Miller, I asked if he'd seen any deer come out of the woods. He said that he had, a buck and a doe, running full speed and too far away for him to shoot.

"Did you shoot?" he asked me.

"Yup, I did," I said proudly. "But the buck was too far away for this old shotgun."

When I saw Pa, he asked the same question. And I gave the same answer. "Buck was just too far away."

In my mind I began to wonder if maybe the deer was too far away. But no amount of thinking would make the deer anything other than lying down. I never told the real story of what happened. It was many years later before I realized that not telling everything is part of becoming a man.

Storytelling

My home community was filled with storytellers, mostly men who could spin a tale that bent you over in laughter or kept you struggling from crying. Some of the stories you remembered because they were such lies that they stuck with you by sheer virtue of their excesses.

Storytelling took place all year long, whenever more than a couple of neighbors got together. But winter, and especially ice fishing, was the ideal time for story sharing.

Starting in early December, sometimes even in late November, Pa, my brothers, and I ice fished on Saturdays and Sundays. During the two-week Christmas break from school we fished every day. We had our pick of lakes—Hills, Round, Norwegian, Gilbert, Pine, Kusel, and Mt. Morris, among others. Our favorite was Mt. Morris, which wasn't a natural lake like the others but a millpond that early settlers had formed by damming a lazy little stream that ran out of Norwegian Lake. Mt. Morris Lake wasn't deep, only twenty to thirty feet at its deepest, but there were lots of weeds and many little bays that made it outstanding for northern pike and bass.

Many of our friends ice fished—we often saw more of them during ice-fishing season than any other time of the year. We fished with tip-ups, devices that could be left alone on the lake while we sat on shore around a little campfire, sharing stories. We spent most of our time huddled around the fire, trying to stay out of the smoke while we watched our tip-ups. On most days, if we got a half-dozen bites all day (a flag on the tip-up flew up when a fish took the bait) that was a lot, so there was plenty of time to just sit and listen to the stories. Everyone had a story to tell.

Someone always had a new story to share, but no one let the new stories get in the way of the old ones. We listened patiently and enjoyed the retelling. No story was ever told in exactly the same way, especially the fish stories, of which there were many. In the fish stories, the weather always got colder, the ice thicker, and the fish bigger with each retelling.

A popular story was about the big northern pike that didn't get away. As we sat around the campfire, someone usually started it off.

"Remember that big northern Murf caught a couple years ago?" Jim Kolka said.

"Weighed twenty pounds, didn't it?"

"It did," my brother Murf said.

"Remember how we had to chop the hole bigger to drag it through the ice?"

"I do," Murf said as he moved a little to get out of the smoke from the fire.

Murf then recounted each detail of the catching, from the size of the minnow he'd used for bait to seeing the monster fish, some forty-two inches long, flopping on the ice. He shared how he had seen the flag on the tip-up jerk up and how he wondered if the wind had blown it loose. He told how the fish had grabbed the minnow and swam only a few feet with it, taking out little line, and how when he took hold of the line the fish tore off so fast he couldn't stop it. He recounted his fear that the fish would take out all the line he had, snap off the minnow, and swim free. But it didn't. It stopped with a yard or two of line remaining. He talked about how he was sweating as he knelt by the hole in the ice, with the cold northwest wind striking him full in the face and the frigid wet fish line numbing his hands.

He recounted how he slowly began pulling in line, hand over hand, the giant fish tugging, straining, jerking. He had only pulled in a few yards of line when the fish dived toward the bottom, the fish line now disappearing between his fingers into the murky depths of the cold water.

There was quiet around the fire as the story was told, only the occasional pop and snap of oak and popple wood as it burned, sending a grayish-blue trickle of smoke upward.

Three times Murf pulled the fish near the hole and three times the fish swam off in a fury. The fourth

time the fish came up into the hole, its mouth—studded with needle-sharp teeth—open, and its dark eyes staring at the fisherman. At this moment, Murf saw clearly that the fish was bigger than the hole and he yelled for someone to fetch the ice chisel.

Jim slowly and carefully chipped the hole larger while Murf held the line tight so the big fish couldn't spit out the hook. Murf shared that he was sure Jim would slip and cut the fish line with the ice chisel. But Jim didn't. In a few minutes, the fish lay on the ice and fishermen from all parts of the lake gathered to gaze at the giant. It was a grand moment for Murf and for everyone who ever dropped a fish line through a hole in a frozen lake. After years of bragging about five-pound fish as big ones, here was a really big one. This was clearly more than a fish story that needed embellishment to hold interest. Here was truth larger than fiction.

Then there was the story of the ice fisherman on a northern Minnesota Lake. His black Labrador dog jumped through an ice hole, swam underneath the ice, and emerged from another fish hole inside of a nearby fish shanty. Fishermen in the shanty swore off drinking after the appearance of the black lab holding a three-pound northern pike in its teeth.

Stories of error and misjudgment were popular, especially if those who experienced the misadventure were present.

"Remember the time you fell in the lake, Jim?" Pa asked. Many in the group had been there and remembered well what had happened. Some began chuckling.

"Don't want to talk about it," Jim said.

Jim had bragged to some of us about how he could walk close to open water and not fall through the ice, that he could tell by sight and sound when the ice was getting thin and wouldn't support him. Everyone knew that ice was fragile close to open water and no one was much interested in checking to see just how thin it was. Except for Jim.

"Recall we had to fish you out of the drink with a popple pole," Pa offered. "Had to cut a tree down cause we couldn't find a dead branch long enough."

"Wasn't a big deal," Jim said. "Water only came up to my waist."

What Jim didn't say was how dangerous it was to

fall into water when the temperature hung around zero. We sat him down by the fire that day, and it took most of the afternoon to dry him out enough so his teeth quit chattering.

Sprinkled with the stories that recounted previous fishing accomplishments were a few that tried to offer words of wisdom to the younger boys in the group.

"You know, don't you, that a Model-T Ford has more power in reverse than in first gear? You get stuck on a hill, just turn the old T around and go up the hill in reverse. I've done it many times." My uncle, Wilbur, shared these words of advice often. No matter that people had long since quit driving Model-T Fords.

John Swendryznski told the tale of the teamster who was especially mindful of his horses.

"Fellow over by Princeton was uncommonly good to his horses. Whenever he hauled a load of grain up that big hill east of town, he would hold a couple of bags of rye on his lap while he sat on the seat. Figured this would lighten the load some for the team."

One of Ray Nelson's favorite stories was about the farmer who bought a horse. The farmer's horse had died and he needed a replacement. He went over to the horse dealer in Wautoma and asked if he had any good draft horses for sale.

"I got some horses for sale," the dealer said. The dealer was known as being shifty, someone not to be trusted. The farmer and the dealer walked over to the corral where there were several horses.

"See that one over there, that big gray horse?" the dealer asked, pointing.

"I see it," the farmer said.

It was a big horse with no apparent blemishes.

"He don't look too good, but he's probably just what you need," the dealer offered.

The farmer thought the horse looked better than average, but he didn't say anything to the dealer, believing he was getting a good deal. He gave the dealer $300 and took the horse home.

When he got the horse in the barnyard, he noticed it bumped into everything. Upon closer inspection, the farmer discovered the horse was blind. He immediately set off to confront the horse dealer.

"You sold me a blind horse," the farmer said angrily.

"Remember, I told you the horse didn't look too good. You bought it anyway."

Today, as I think back to those times on Mt. Morris lake, I remember bitter cold and balmy thaws when water accumulated on the ice. I remember when the ice snapped and cracked as it contracted— Pa said it was talking to us. And I remember when it snowed so hard you sometimes had difficulty finding your way from your tip-up on the lake back to the campfire on shore.

There would be long breaks in the storytelling as we all watched the snow and the campfire. Each snowflake sizzled a little when it hit the flames and melted. Then someone would start up again, usually with "Do you remember when?"

Morty

His real name was Mortimer Oliphant, but everyone called him Morty Elephant. Morty was no one to correct you when you mispronounced his name. He had such a speech impediment that you couldn't gather if he was pronouncing his name like he wanted you to or telling you something about the weather. Unfortunately, most people didn't try to figure out what Morty was saying, except for Pa. Pa tried to understand him and did pretty well at it, better than most people in our community.

Morty lived about two miles from our farm, in a place called Skunk's Hollow. No one really knew the source of the community's name, other than the farms there were tucked in and around some little lakes that could be called hollows. I doubted there were any more skunks in Skunk's Hollow than elsewhere in the area.

Morty lived alone on a sandy, hilly eighty-acre farm that barely grew enough crops to feed his handful of skinny Guernsey cows. He had never taken much to modern conveniences such as tractors or electricity. As long as I knew him he farmed with horses, lit his tiny house with kerosene lamps, and pumped water with a gasoline engine. Morty had little contact with people, except when he drove his old '28 Chevrolet to town for groceries. This he did once a month or so; the rest of the time he stayed home. Folks who didn't know about his speech problem and tried to talk with him were quickly put off because he sputtered and spit and made quite a spectacle of himself just to fire off a few words. And then the words might as well have been in another language. In fact, some people thought Morty didn't speak English but was talking Norwegian or maybe Polish.

Pa would drive down to see Morty ever so often because he knew Morty never got to talk to anybody, and besides he might be sick or hurt and not able to take care of himself. He had no telephone to let anyone know if he got into trouble, and even if he did no one could understand what he was saying.

It was a cool day in October when Pa asked if I wanted to ride down and check on Morty. I said I would because people sometimes talked about him, and although I had only seen him a few times, I had never heard him speak. Kids in school said he was strange and kind of weird and you ought never go near him because there was no telling what he would do to you.

I crawled into our '36 Plymouth and we drove along the country road until it turned west, and then in just a quarter-mile or so we came to Morty's farm. It was the kind of place that people called "run down." Rusty farm machinery littered the yard. A horse-drawn disk sat by the corncrib, grown over with grass and weeds. A walking plow leaned against the wagon shed. The remnants of a rusty grain binder stood abandoned near the barn, and a high-wheeled, wooden-spoked wagon was parked next to the binder. The way the machinery was scattered about, it looked as if Morty had driven his team to a particular spot, unhitched the horses, and then forgot the implement until the next time he wanted to use it.

Tall grass grew everywhere. Morty's dog, Ralph, had beaten a few trails through the tangled vegetation in search of a rabbit or maybe a rat that had been raiding the corncrib. At least that's how I figured what had happened.

Ralph came out to the car. He was an old black dog with gray hairs around his muzzle and a hoarse bark that announced our arrival. His tail flopped back and forth when he recognized Pa's car.

Morty's house was best named a cabin because it was only one story and appeared to have only two or three rooms. A rusty stovepipe stuck out of the roof, and a trail of wood smoke lazied off toward the barn.

The door of the cabin eased open, and a gray-haired, skinny old man, wearing faded bib overalls and a flannel shirt with holes in the elbows, squinted out toward us.

"At you, Hoirm?" Morty asked.

"How are ya, Morty?" Pa asked by way of greeting.

Morty said something in response that I couldn't understand, and he beckoned with his hand that we should come inside. Earlier, Pa had told me I shouldn't be surprised by what I saw in the house because Morty was a bachelor and didn't take much to housecleaning and keeping things in order.

The house was dark inside, but pleasantly warm. It smelled of wood smoke. When my eyes adjusted to the darkness, I saw that we were in the kitchen, a good-sized room with a table, a cook-stove, some shelves nailed to the wall, a sink with a drainpipe that stuck through the wall, and a calendar hanging from a nail near the door. Dirty dishes were piled on one side of the table. A sooty coffeepot rattled on top of the stove; a little curl of steam lifted from its spout. Beyond the smell of wood smoke and coffee, I detected another smell but couldn't tell what it was.

"Well, how you feelin'?" Pa asked.

"Hitty god," Morty answered, which must have meant "pretty good."

Pa had understood, and the conversation went on. Usually Morty answered in single words, sometimes two words. I didn't have any idea what he was saying, even though I could see he was trying as hard as he could to be understood. I could see why he put off people. As he tried to spit out words, his long white hair flew around in every direction; his whiskered chin jumped up and down, and deep furrows appeared in his forehead. I'm sure he had no idea how gruesome he looked when he talked.

"Jerol'," he said, looking at me. I understood my name.

"Got a pet-toon," he said, trying to speak as carefully as he could.

"What?" I replied.

"Got a pet-toon," he repeated. It sounded something like "I've got a spittoon." I looked around to see if I could see one, but I didn't.

"He says he's got a pet raccoon," Pa translated, "and he's wondering if you'd like to see it."

"Sure," I said. I now knew the source of the extra smell.

Morty gave a soft whistle, and from back in the corner of the kitchen, behind a wooden box, a full-grown raccoon emerged. The raccoon walked right up to Morty and stopped in front of him.

"Ni lil 'toon," Morty said. "Ni lil 'toon." The raccoon cocked its head to one side and made a chattering kind of noise in response to Morty's unintelligible words. Morty continued talking to the raccoon. The raccoon seemed to comprehend every word as it sat there listening and talking back in raccoon language. I'd never seen anything like it. Somewhere I had read that certain people have the ability to talk with wild animals, and here I was seeing it happen.

"Ga a ager, ta," Morty said.

"He says he's got a badger," Pa said. I knew about badgers. They were mean. Pa said that when a badger tangled with a farm dog, the badger usually won.

Morty shuffled over to the side of the kitchen and lifted up a floorboard, exposing a crawl space. The cabin did not have a basement. This time Morty made a kind of clicking noise with his teeth. Pa and I stood next to Morty, staring down into the space under the kitchen, but I couldn't see anything. Morty clicked his teeth again. I caught the glimpse of something moving, a large animal. It was clearly a badger. I could see the stripes down its face when the light struck it.

"He don li fks," Morty said.

"Morty said the badger doesn't like other people," Pa translated.

Later Pa told me that the badger lived under the cabin and came right up into the kitchen for Morty's handouts. I was wondering how the raccoon and the badger got along, living in the same house. And I wondered how Ralph, the old black dog, got along with the both of them. I figured that each had its own territory, with the badger claiming the region under the kitchen, the raccoon having its box in the corner, and the rest of the place belonging to Ralph.

While we were driving home, Pa told me about Morty's pet flying squirrel, which we had not seen.

When Morty drove to town for groceries, he carried the flying squirrel under his shirt. He liked to walk up to a stranger, open his shirt a little, and allow the flying squirrel to stick out its head. Most strangers, especially tourists from the city, would jump back in terror. Morty would laugh with a kind of cackle that only succeeded in painting him as more eccentric then he really was.

We continued visiting Morty every so often. Then one day we heard that he had been found dead in his kitchen. Most people didn't seem to care that he had died. But I know that his pet badger, flying squirrel, and raccoon surely did. And I wondered what they would have told us about Morty, if they had been able to talk to us the way they had talked to him.

Stormy

"Ann's calf will be yours," Pa said. We were milking cows one May evening and the comment came without any previous discussion. "Its seems right for you to have a little more pay for your summer work. Ann's calf will be it."

I was thrilled beyond words. My very own calf. I could raise the heifer calf as a 4-H project, and when it was grown she would become my first cow. That's how Pa started his dairy herd, with one cow. I could do the same. I couldn't wait for the calf's birth. Ann was due in January.

On a January evening nine months later, snow was swirling around the corner of the barn and drifting in front of the door, making it nearly impossible for me to yank it open. It was evening milking time and Pa, as was his routine, had come out to the barn a little earlier than me with the milk cans. He hadn't been ahead of me by more than fifteen minutes and already his tracks in the snow had disappeared. The snow had stopped around suppertime, just before dark. Now, an hour later, the wind had come up from the northwest, and the temperature had begun falling—typical for a mid-January storm.

I kicked aside the snow, carefully holding the kerosene lantern in one hand, until I could crack open the door enough to squeeze through. The warmth of the barn was inviting, a pleasant contrast to the weather outside. The cattle stood quietly in their stanchions eating corn silage as they waited to be milked. Along with the warmth and the quiet there was a fusion of smells—the sharp smell of corn silage mixed with the subtle aroma of fresh oat straw and the pungent odor of cow manure.

I hung my lantern on a nail behind the cows and

walked to the far end of the barn, where the horses stood in their stalls and the calves were bouncing around in their pen. Pa had just forked hay into the horse mangers.

"Stormy night," I said.

"Yup," Pa answered. Sometimes Pa didn't say much. But often you could tell his meaning by the expression on his face. Tonight he looked concerned.

"See anything different about Ann?" he asked. Ann was a big, mostly white Holstein that stood about halfway in the lineup of fifteen cows that made up our milking herd.

"Nope," I answered. I didn't want to admit that I hadn't even looked at Ann, or for that matter any of the other cows, as I had walked down the aisle back of them.

"Looks like she'll freshen tonight," Pa said, as he hung the pitchfork in its place on the wall back of the cows.

I walked back down the aisle and stopped behind Ann. She was fidgeting a little, and she hadn't eaten much of her silage.

"Could be," I said, not being able to predict near as well as Pa when an animal would give birth. I was excited beyond words. Ann's calf was going to be my calf.

We each took our milk stools from their hooks, grabbed milk pails, and began milking. Pa milked the hard-milking cows and those that were a little skittish and sometimes kicked. I milked the easy ones.

An hour later, with milking finished, we stopped to look at Ann once more before leaving for the house.

"We'll check her before we go to bed," Pa said. He said it matter-of-factly. During his years on the farm he had assisted many cows that were giving birth.

The wind had gone down some when Pa and I returned to the barn later that evening. A sliver of a cold moon hung in a clear black sky. Pa carried a lantern that cast long shadows over the snowdrifts that had piled up against the side of the barn. The temperature was still dropping. I could feel the cold on my ears and hear it as my boots crunched on the snow.

It was warm in the barn, and quiet. Most of the cows were lying down, chewing their cuds, but not

Ann. She lay on her side, breathing rather unevenly. Pa hung the lantern on a nail and stooped down for a closer look. I was surprised to see two white feet sticking out from under her tail—she had started to give birth.

Pa grabbed up some loose straw and spread it out back of Ann.

"Run to the house and fetch a pail of hot soapy water," Pa said. "Looks like Ann's gonna need a little help."

When I returned with the water, Pa washed his hands and arms and instructed me to do the same. From somewhere he had gotten a thin rope about six or eight feet long.

"I'll go in for a look," Pa said, shoving his hand in around the protruding legs up to his elbow.

"Everything feels OK," Pa said, "The head's right there. It's an awful big calf. That's why Ann's havin' some trouble. Grab hold a foot; I'll grab the other."

I did as I was told. The foot was wet and slippery and hard to hold.

"When I say so, pull. Gentle, don't jerk, just pull steady."

Pa paused. "Now," he said.

Ann was straining as we pulled, but nothing happened. When she quit straining, the feet seemed to suck back inside her.

"That's not workin'," Pa said. "We'll try the rope."

He tied a slipknot around each foot and handed me part of the rope while he held the other part.

"When she strains, we'll pull. We'll see if this works."

I held the rope and waited. One of the barn cats moseyed by, curious about what was going on.

"OK, pull," Pa said. "But easy."

We both pulled and the feet emerged farther than they had before.

"Look at the size of those front legs," Pa said. "You got yourself quite a calf here."

Ann mooed softly as she strained. With each effort, we pulled a little more, not allowing the calf to slip backward. Soon we saw the calf's nose.

"Your calf's got a black nose," Pa said as we continued pulling, waiting for Ann to strain. Sweat beaded on my forehead and I could see Pa sweating, too. His shirt was soaked. We couldn't rest though, couldn't allow the rope to go slack or what we'd gained would be lost.

My arms ached as time went by.

"I can't hold on much longer," I said. "My arms are killing me."

"You can't let go . . . won't be long now. Just keep pulling steady and when she strains, pull harder." Pa said. He wiped his bare arm against his forehead, removing some of the sweat.

I could see the calf's forehead emerge, and then the entire head was out.

"Beautiful calf, Jerold," Pa said. The head lay against the front feet, the ears back.

"Just the shoulders left, just the shoulders. Keep pullin'."

Ann gave a mighty strain and both Pa and I pulled as hard as we could. With a swoosh, the front shoulders emerged and then the rest of the calf.

"Got yourself a bull," Pa said. "A big one, too. Bet he'll go a hundred pounds."

"But I wanted a heifer," I said, bitterly disappointed. "I wanted a heifer calf—the beginning of my own herd of cows."

"You take what you get," Pa said. "And you got a mighty fine bull calf."

Pa grabbed some empty burlap bags used for cow feed and began rubbing the little bull dry. Already the calf was holding up his head and shaking it back and forth.

Ann looked around and lowed softly at her new calf.

Later, as we walked to the house, Pa said, "You look like you lost your last friend."

"I was hoping for a heifer calf," I said. "Had my heart set on a heifer and then this big bull comes along."

"Don't always get what you want," Pa said. "Sometimes it's for the better. You never know, this may be one of those times."

I didn't say anything as I walked with my head down, kicking clumps of snow with my boot.

"What're you gonna name that little fella?" Pa asked.

I hadn't even thought about a name. I had a heifer's name all picked out. I was gonna call a heifer Sue. I always liked that name. I hadn't even considered a bull's name.

"I don't know," I grumbled.

The next day, while we were doing the chores, Pa asked me again about a name for my bull calf. I didn't answer. I knew I'd never like that calf. I thought, When he grows up, I'll sell him and earn a couple hundred dollars. That seemed like a lot of money and I began thinking about all the things I could buy.

Finally I said, "Think I'll name him Stormy. He was born during a big storm."

"That's a good name," Pa replied. The little bull was looking at us from his bed of knee-deep oat straw.

Stormy grew rapidly. He learned how to drink from a pail on the second try and just kept on growing. By early May, when he was four-and-a-half months old, he was one of the biggest calves in the pen, bigger than heifer calves that were a month or two older. By now Stormy and I had become acquainted, but were a long way from becoming friends. In the back of my mind I was still disappointed I hadn't gotten a heifer. I had Stormy out of the barn several times. As my 4-H project, I had begun teaching him to lead with a rope and halter. I prac-

ticed leading him two or three times a week and discovered how stubborn he was. He would either refuse to move, or he insisted on going where he wanted to go, with me dragging along behind. I didn't like Stormy, but kept working at teaching him to lead. To sell him, he had to lead. Progress was slow, but we were making progress. Until the big spring windstorm.

When I got out to the barn that morning in early May, I noticed that the sky was red in the east and a bank of fierce-looking clouds was building in the west. This in itself was not unusual, for spring thundershowers often gave these signs.

"Think we're in for a bad one," Pa said. "Air doesn't feel right."

A soft breeze was blowing from the west when we walked to the house for breakfast. New leaves were pushing out on the elm tree that stood near the kitchen porch and there was green grass on the south side of the house. A meadowlark called from the field by the road. It sure didn't feel like stormy weather to me.

But the wind got stronger all day, and when I got home from school that afternoon, the howl of the wind was everywhere. The straw stack back of the barn—what was left of it after providing cattle bedding all winter—was scattered across the yard. Small tree limbs had blown off the elm tree near the kitchen porch, and a larger tree limb had cracked off the apple tree in the front yard.

Pa didn't say much about the storm as we ate supper, but I could see concern etched on his face. We all knew about windstorm damage on the farm, to early crops, to trees, and to farm buildings.

In the barn for the evening milking, I noticed that the animals were uneasy, sensing the storm raging outside. Frank and Charlie, our draft horses, pawed the floor in their stalls. The cattle were not eating as much as usual. Fanny, our dog, lay back of the cows, her head resting on her paws and her ears up. Obviously, she could hear the wind and sense the power of the storm.

Stormy, my bull calf, seemed his usual self. He bounced around the calf pen and trotted over to lick my hand when I approached. I scratched his head. He liked it when I did that.

It was still daylight when I crawled up the hay-mow ladder to pitch down hay for the cattle. Upstairs in the near-empty barn, the sounds of the storm were everywhere. Oak beams creaked and cracked, and the big doors through which we hauled loads of hay rattled and shuddered with each gust of wind. Usually, the haymow was a quiet, peaceful place, filled with the cooing of pigeons and the soothing sound of breezes blowing outside. But this evening the haymow was a place of frightening, ear-splitting sounds, as the barn stood tall in the wind and protested every gust.

In bed that night, I heard the relentless wind screaming around the corners of the house. With each gust, the window glass rattled.

I awakened in the dull dawn of morning to Pa's shouting.

"Come quick! The barn's tipping over! The barn's tipping over!"

I grabbed up my clothes and ran along the long hallway and down the stairs to the dining room. Ma was there to greet me.

"Go help your Pa. The barn's going over," Ma said with fright written all over her face. She was cranking the telephone, many small rings (a general ring it was called) to inform the neighbors that we needed help.

"This is Eleanor Apps. The wind is blowing over our barn!" I heard Ma scream into the phone. "The wind is blowing over our barn!"

I met Pa at the barn door. He was gagging on his false teeth, which didn't fit just right and loosened when he was excited.

"West wall is down. Calves buried. Beam's layin' on top of the cows. Whole thing is goin' over. When it goes, it will kill everything. Help me with the beam."

Together we dragged the huge oak beam off the backs of the cows. Its weight had knocked several cows to the floor.

"Start lettin' out cows," Pa yelled.

I began opening stanchions on one end of the barn, the part of the barn that still seemed intact, and Pa worked on the other end, the section that was likely to topple any minute.

Cows were bellowing, the horses were rearing in their stalls, the herd bull, with part of the barn wall collapsed around him, was roaring in a fearful rage, and the calves, some of them buried to their necks,

bawled in pain. Above the sound of disaster was the howl of the wind, the never-ending wind that had blown since the previous day without stopping.

As I opened stanchions and yelled at the cows to leave, swatting them on the rumps to offer further encouragement, I glanced at the calf pen, hoping to spot Stormy. All that I saw was broken barn wall and parts of calves.

Finally, with the cows outside—two of them were badly injured and limped through the door to the barnyard—I ran to the calf pen in search of Stormy. I first encountered one of the heifer calves, buried except for its head. The animal was dead.

I found Stormy in the far corner of the pen, his head covered with loose hay and his back half-buried in rubble. I uncovered his head. He was still alive, but the spirited look in his eyes was gone.

"Pa, I need help with the calves!" I yelled.

Pa was untying the horses and leading them out the door. Frantically, I clawed at the broken cement blocks that had been part of the barn wall and dug at the dirt that had buried my calf. Pa arrived and helped me free Stormy and drag him out of the pen to the

outside. Stormy couldn't stand and he was breathing with great difficulty.

I returned to the calves. Two were completely buried and dead.

"Leave the dead ones," Pa yelled. "Uncover those that are alive."

Before we had uncovered the last calf, John and Roman Macijeski, our neighbors to the east, arrived and began helping. Two calves were only scratched and bruised. John and Roman helped construct a makeshift pen to hold the calves a safe distance from the doomed barn.

Pa crawled over the rubble and untied our herd bull that stood with his head down, bellowing loudly. Pa led him by his ring and tied him to a fence post a safe distance from the barn.

"I think if we brace the barn, we'll save it from tipping anymore," John Macijeski said. From an earlier building project, we had saved some railroad ties, which we quickly piled up under the east end of the barn to brace it. By the time we were half through the bracing, more than twenty men had arrived—our neighbors pitching in to help.

"Unless the wind gets any stronger, I think this will do it," John said.

We now looked at what had happened. The barn had been pushed more than six feet off of its foundation, toppling the west basement wall, which had buried the calves and loosened the beam that fell on the cows.

With the barn somewhat stabilized I rushed to the makeshift calf pen and Stormy. He was lying on fresh straw, which someone had placed in the pen. His neck was stretched out and his eyes closed. I put his head on my lap and rubbed his neck. He opened his eyes, but they were cloudy and he didn't seem to see me.

John Macijeski walked over to the pen.

"That your calf?" John asked.

"It is," I answered, trying to keep the tears back.

"Looks like his back's broken. I think we ought to put him out of his misery. Be best," John said.

John had found a hammer and was poised to strike the calf in the head.

"Wait," I said.

"No sense waiting, Jerry. Your calf probably has a

broken back. Look. The poor little thing can't even hold up his head."

"But he's my 4-H project, and then I was going to sell him," I said. "You can't kill my 4-H project."

"It's the best thing," John said quietly.

Just then Pa came by.

"Don't let him kill my calf," I said.

Pa looked at John and then at the calf.

"We'll take care of the calf later," Pa said.

The next day, when we were trying to put things back in order and continue the clean up, Stormy was still alive, but barely.

"Probably should put your calf out of its misery," Pa said.

But I could see a spark of life in Stormy's eyes that no one else had seen. And he was looking at me in a way that only I could understand.

"Just a few more days," I pleaded. "I know Stormy will get better." It was at that moment that I understood how I felt about Stormy. Something I didn't think I wanted had turned out to be what I wanted most.

"A few more days," Pa said.

From that day on, Stormy and I developed a special relationship. I nursed him back to health, and by July he was walking again.

Uncle Charlie

Uncle Charlie was lazy. Pa said he was the laziest man he'd ever met. Uncle Charlie and Aunt Sophie vacationed at our farm two weeks every summer, usually in July. He really was my great uncle, as his wife, Sophie, was my grandmother's sister. But calling him Great Uncle Charlie seemed too much of a mouthful, so Uncle Charlie it was.

Uncle Charlie lived in Milwaukee, where he sold life insurance. One of my mother's cousins claimed he followed pregnant women home so he could write insurance on their unborn children, but that fact has never been substantiated. Pa didn't believe the story. He didn't think Uncle Charlie had enough gumption to follow anybody anywhere.

Nevertheless, the dog days of summer sent Uncle Charlie and Aunt Sophie north for two weeks. Aunt Sophie was good help for my mother. We were usually in the midst of haying season so there were many meals to fix, piles of dirty clothes to wash, a garden to look after, chickens to feed, and eggs to gather. Aunt Sophie helped with all these tasks and seemed to enjoy doing them.

Uncle Charlie was no help whatsoever. He knew nothing about farming and had no inclination to learn. For Uncle Charlie, vacation meant sitting outside in a rocking chair, and that's what he did, every day. After breakfast, he found a shady place under the big old elm tree between the house and the barn, and there he parked until it was time to eat.

Besides coming in the house to eat, the only other time he moved was when the sun moved. He followed the shade around the tree from morning to late afternoon. Nothing besides the hot sun and meals caused him to lift out of his chair.

One hot afternoon, when we were driving a huge load of loose hay from the field to the barn, Pa spotted Uncle Charlie sitting right in the center of the driveway, which was a shady place. There was no way Pa could steer the team and the load of hay around Uncle Charlie.

As we approached him, Pa yelled out, "Uncle Charlie, you're gonna have to move."

He didn't budge. I was riding on the load of hay with Pa. The driveway was quite a steep incline so I knew Pa didn't want to stop the team mid-hill. Pa yelled again. "Charlie, damn it, move."

Pa never thought much of Uncle Charlie; in fact, he cared little for anyone who didn't want to work. For Pa, work meant physical labor. Reluctantly, Uncle Charlie dragged his rocking chair out of the way as the load of hay brushed by him.

Uncle Charlie had one redeeming characteristic, at least in the eyes of my brothers and me. He knew how to make kites. We looked forward to his visits because we knew that after a couple of days of rocking under the shade tree, he would inquire about some old newspapers, some flour and water, a peach box, and a roll of store string. He never said what he was going to build, but each year he constructed a beautiful kite. Our guess was he didn't know how to build anything else, but that really didn't matter because we always marveled at his kites and what they could do. The kite making usually started at noon, while we all rested under Uncle Charlie's shade tree, as it was known during the two weeks of his visit.

"Say, Jerold, you got any old newspapers around here and maybe a peach crate?" Uncle Charlie would say. He wore a straw hat, the kind that people wore in stage shows—flat on top and with a stiff brim, not at all like the straw hats we wore out to the hay field, which had a tall crown and a flexible brim that we could adjust.

I had anticipated his question from the time when Aunt Sophie's letter arrived announcing they'd be coming. I ran to the woodshed where I had squirreled away the necessary materials for a kite.

"Here's what you need," I said, a broad grin spread across my face, as I handed the materials to Uncle Charlie. He rather deliberately looked over the newspaper, unfolding a section and tugging at it.

I'd wondered if newspapers came in different strengths, but I don't recall that Uncle Charlie ever rejected any newspaper I'd ever handed him as being of inferior quality. Next he inspected the wooden peach box, examining each of the thin boards.

"These will do," he finally announced with great authority in his voice. He retrieved a thin jackknife from his pocket and snapped open a tiny blade. I'd never seen such a small jackknife. Pa's knife was three times the size of Uncle Charlie's. But I suspected that insurance salesmen didn't have much call for a jack-knife, at least they didn't use one as often as a farmer. A farmer used his jackknife every day, for cutting binder twine to digging a sliver out of his finger. I couldn't quite imagine to what use a Milwaukee insurance agent might put a pocketknife, maybe slic-ing open a letter or cutting an insurance form apart, but this was only conjecture.

"I'll need a hammer to knock this peach box apart," Uncle Charlie announced.

I ran for a hammer, and this time remembered to bring along the ball of store string we'd saved from Uncle Charlie's last visit.

"Ah, good, you brought the string, too," Uncle Charlie said, as he rubbed his hands together and then spit on one before picking up the hammer. I'd seen woodsmen spit on their hands before taking up an ax, but I'd never seen anyone spit on his hands before using a hammer, not even a carpenter. Maybe this was the way they did it in the city; I didn't know.

Gently, Uncle Charlie knocked the thin boards off the thicker ones that formed the ends of the peach box. Again he carefully inspected the thin boards, and then selected one. As he worked, my brothers and I sat watching, not saying a word. Uncle Charlie never said much, and it made no sense to interrupt him while he was engaged in such an important task. Carefully, he sliced the thin boards into long strips about a quarter inch wide. One strip was about twenty-four inches long; the other was maybe eighteen inch-es long. He made two or three sets of thinly-sliced wooden strips.

"Never can tell, we might have an accident and need some repair strips," he said. He tied the longer and the shorter strips of wood together with string so they looked like a cross.

Uncle Charlie held the crossed strips of wood away from him, inspecting them from every angle. Finally he announced, "I think this will work."

He took the newspaper, laid it out on the grass and placed the wooden framework on it. He moved the framework this way and that and finally called for scissors, which I placed in his hand. He was in deep concentration, like I imagined a surgeon would be when he requested an instrument.

Carefully, Uncle Charlie cut out the newspaper a couple inches larger than the frame. Anticipating his next request, I had gotten a bowl with some water.

"Time to mix the paste," he announced. He poured some flour into the water, stirring it with a leftover wooden stick. He poured and stirred, poured and stirred, occasionally lifting the stick from the mixture to test its consistency. He seemed to take forever to do what I considered the simplest of tasks.

"It must be just right," he said as he worked. More pouring, more stirring. More stirring, more pouring. Finally, when my patience had all but vanished, he began smearing the paste along the edges of the newspaper, making certain that each section received just the right amount. With the paste applied, he ever so carefully folded the newspaper over the frame, tugging a little here, pushing a little there, until the newspaper fit firm and snug against the frame.

"Well, that's it for now," Uncle Charlie said as he looked up from his work. "Put this someplace safe so it can dry, and we'll finish it tomorrow. And if the wind's right, we'll give it a trial flight." Uncle Charlie tipped his hat over his eyes and seemed immediately to fall asleep. I decided that kite making, especially the way that Uncle Charlie did it, must be exhausting work.

I could hardly wait for the next day to arrive. As usual, that afternoon Uncle Charlie sat under the big shade tree, moving his rocking chair about every half-hour. I didn't care, for I knew that tomorrow great and exciting things were to occur—mysterious happenings during which a piece of newspaper and peach-box sticks would fly, would soar like a hawk.

That night, when the chores were finished and I lay in bed, I thought about kites from other years and how they climbed and swooped and pulled on the kite string like a northern pike on a fish line. I hoped the weather would be sunny and the wind just right, not too strong, not too light.

I was usually out in the hay field before Uncle Charlie crawled out of bed in the morning. This was another of Uncle Charlie's habits that Pa absolutely despised. Anyone not up by 5:30 or 6 a.m. was the closest thing to worthless that Pa knew. Not getting up in time for breakfast increased even more Uncle Charlie's negative status.

But I thought Uncle Charlie was wonderful. Here was a man who knew how to do something that Pa didn't know how to do, or never took time to do. Here was a man who knew how to build kites and fly them, too.

The day dawned clear and warm, with a light breeze blowing from the southwest. It was a great day for haymaking and for kite flying. Pa, my brothers, and I were out in the hay field shortly after breakfast, pitching hay on the steel-wheeled hay wagon and hauling the loads to the barn for storage.

As usual, Uncle Charlie sat under the shade tree, his flat-topped straw hat tipped over his eyes.

"Hey, Charlie, working hard?" Pa said as we walked past him on the way to dinner. Startled, Uncle Charlie's head snapped up and a sheepish grin spread across his face.

"Yup," he answered. For all his lazy tendencies, Uncle Charlie was good-natured and truly one who enjoyed his vacation time.

Hurriedly I ate, anticipating finishing our kite before once more going out to the hay field. Uncle Charlie seemed in no hurry at all. I was certain he had forgotten all about the kite. My brothers and I knew it was not good manners to bring up a task that someone was doing for us, particularly when he was on vacation, so we merely glanced at each other, wondering if Uncle Charlie had remembered.

" 'Spect we'd better get at our project," he finally said as he pushed back from the table. I rushed out to the woodshed and retrieved the partially completed kite from where I had placed it to dry. I handed it to Uncle Charlie, who inspected it carefully, running his fingers over the glued parts, examining the tightness of the paper over the frame.

"Looks pretty good," he said. I breathed a sigh of relief.

A couple of years ago, at this moment in the kite-constructing process, Uncle Charlie declared the partially made kite absolutely inferior and we started with fresh newspaper and lost a day in the process.

With his jackknife blade, he punched tiny holes in the newspaper on either side of the frame, near the top and the bottom and close to either side.

"Got to have a good harness for the kite," he said as he wet the end of a piece of string with his tongue and pushed it through the hole, around the frame, and back through the second hole, where he firmly tied it.

When he was finished, a piece of string was tied firmly to the top and bottom of the kite and another from side to side. The strings crossed in the middle, about two inches away from the kite. Carefully Uncle Charlie tied the end of the string from the ball to the harness.

"One thing more we need," Uncle Charlie said. "Go ask your Ma for some old rags. We need a tail for this kite."

Shortly I returned with a handful of discarded dish towels, socks that were beyond repair, and a holey pair of Pa's long underwear.

"Don't think we'll need the underwear," Uncle Charlie said, grinning. "Old dish towels ought to do it."

Apparently a kite's tail is less fussy to construct than any other part of the kite. Uncle Charlie grabbed up the worn-out towels, tore them into strips without so much as giving them a second glance, and in a couple of minutes announced that the tail was ready. He tied about six feet of rags onto the bottom of the kite.

"Well, that's it," he said "I think she's ready to fly."

For some reason, when a kite was finished it moved from being an "it" to a "she" for Uncle Charlie.

"Let's see what she'll do, boys," Uncle Charlie said as he proudly carried his creation to the recently cut hay field, just across the road from the house. I carried the ball of string and my brothers carried the extra rags for the tail, in case more might be needed.

Uncle Charlie instructed me to unwind several yards of store string from the ball we had been saving all year, from string wrapped around groceries and other things Ma had bought at the mercantile store. We had a ball of string as big as a softball.

I held the kite string, Murf held the extra rags for the tail, and Duck carried the string ball, ready to unwind it.

The time of reckoning had arrived. Would this year's kite fly like those of other years? It was one of the most exciting moments of our summer, right up there with the Fourth of July and swimming in Chain O' Lake.

Uncle Charlie held the new kite high over his head, instructing me to tighten the string. "When I yell, you start running with the string," Uncle Charlie said.

As I held the string, my heart pounded in anticipation.

"Run, Jerold!" Uncle Charlie said. Duck, with the ball of string, raced alongside me as I ran sideways, watching the kite leave Uncle Charlie's hands.

"Run faster!" Uncle Charlie yelled. I took off across the hay field; Duck kept with me stride for stride. The kite was now twenty or thirty feet in the air and climbing, going higher as I ran.

"Let out more string," Uncle Charlie instructed.

I stopped running and allowed a few yards of string to slip through my fingers. The kite shuddered and stopped climbing, and then slowly began falling.

"Run again!" yelled Uncle Charlie. Duck and I ran and the kite resumed its climb.

By now we had run a third of the way across the hay field. It was like running around our school softball diamond a dozen times at top speed, something you didn't ordinarily do. My side was starting to hurt and I was out of breath. Duck was red in the face, but he wasn't complaining.

"You can stop running now," shouted Uncle Charlie. "Let out some more string, but easy, a little at a time."

As the string slowly slipped through my fingers, the kite continued climbing. It wobbled a little and the rag tail swung back and forth like the pendulum of a clock. It was alive in my hands, gently tugging on the string. Few experiences compare to holding onto a kite string with the kite soaring as high as the clouds, swaying as the wind direction shifted.

"Ain't she a beauty?" Uncle Charlie said. He held his flat straw hat in front of him as he looked skyward. "Ain't that kite just about the prettiest thing you'd ever see?" he continued. He was smiling broadly. Slowly, I continued letting out string, yard by yard. The kite grew increasingly smaller until it was no larger than a small bird, but it continued climbing, the tail slowly swaying back and forth.

Memories are not clear as to exactly what happened next. Depending on which witness to the event you ask, you'll receive a different answer. My version is Duck wasn't watching the ball of string carefully enough and he let all the string off the ball. It slipped through my fingers and then there was no more string and the kite was on its own. My brother Murf, who held the extra rags for the tail, claimed that I had been jerking on the string to make the kite dance and the string broke.

No matter how it happened, it happened. The kite was free as the birds in the sky around it. It climbed until it was out of sight.

"That was a good kite, boys," Uncle Charlie said. "A really good one."

Fanny

"For sale. Purebred collie puppies. Ten dollars each. Will ship by rail to all points in the Midwest," read the ad in the farm paper.

Our farm dog, Rex, had grown old and slept most of the time. He would raise his head when a car drove into the farmyard, bark once or twice feebly, but he wouldn't get up from his resting place under the box elder tree that stood just west of the woodshed.

After Pa saw the ad, he said he was ordering one of the pups. "Rex just can't do his job anymore," Pa said.

"Don't you tell anybody that I paid $10 for a puppy. Neighbors would say it was an outlandish price."

Most of our neighbors had mixed-breed dogs that they got for nothing. Some neighbor dog was always having puppies, the result of a late-night intimacy between neighborhood dogs. The lineage of these puppies was a mystery, but "Who cared?" was the common view. A dog is a dog, isn't it?

Pa cared. Somewhere he had heard about collie dogs, about their skill with cattle and as all-around farm dogs. Rex was a mixed breed, some German shepherd, some collie, but mostly mystery. Pa described Rex as a so-so dog. Not the worst but a long way from the best. He wanted something better.

A few days later the phone rang. It was the railroad depot agent.

"Got a pup here for you, Herman," he said.

Pa backed the '36 Plymouth out of the garage and headed for town. In a half-hour, he was back with a wooden crate containing a little collie pup.

"Ain't she a beauty?" Pa said.

"Cute little thing," Ma said. "But you sure this pup's worth $10? Buy a lot of boy's clothes for $10."

Pa didn't answer her. He was busy removing boards from the crate and humming a little tune.

"Think I'll name her Fanny," Pa said. "It's a good name for a dog."

The pup had big alert eyes, a long nose, and a tail that began wagging the moment she saw us. She was brown and tan with a white stripe down her nose.

"Find her a bowl of milk," Pa instructed.

The little collie pushed her nose in the milk clear up to her eyes. She pulled it out as quickly as she pushed it in, with a kind of a why-did-I-do-that look on her face.

The pup grew rapidly. Like other pups she was into all sorts of mischief. One day Ma found her in the chicken house, chasing chickens off their nests and causing all kinds of commotion. Ma got to the chicken house just in the nick of time because a huge leghorn rooster had had enough of the pup's foolishness and had driven the little collie into a corner and was pecking her on the head.

Another day, Ma had finished washing and hanging the clothes on the clothesline out back of the house. The pup watched Pa's overalls flapping in the wind until she couldn't contain herself. She leaped in the air, trying to catch a pant leg as it floated by. To her surprise, she caught it in her mouth and to her even greater surprise managed to jerk the overalls from the line.

Ma spotted the little collie vigorously shaking the overalls like it was killing some wild animal. Few things the pup could have done that would have been worse. Washing clothes was hard work, and now Ma would have to rewash Pa's overalls and even sew up a couple of holes Fanny had torn in one of the legs.

"Herm," Ma said at the dinner table. Pa, my brothers, and I knew that when Ma used that tone of voice there was trouble. And nobody wanted trouble with Ma.

"Do you knew what your pup did this morning?" At times like this there was no doubt about the new pup's ownership.

"Nope," Pa said. He really knew because he had been working in the granary and had caught a glimpse of Ma taking the overalls away from Fanny, but he wanted to hear Ma's version of the terrible deed.

"That pup of yours just about chewed up a pair of

your best overalls."

"Is that right?" Pa answered. He was trying to busy himself with eating dinner.

"You're gonna have to tie up that pup," Ma said.

"Ah, let's give her another chance. Just a pup, you know. A puppy with any spunk will get in some trouble, and Fanny's got lots of spunk."

"One more trick like this and I'll tie her up myself," Ma said. She was getting red in the face.

"I'll keep an eye on her," Pa said, trying to diffuse what could become a difficult situation. My brothers and I sat quietly, eating and not taking sides in this discussion. It was always interesting to see how Pa worked his way out of difficult situations with Ma.

Fanny got into trouble about once a week, and the discussion around the table was always the same. Ma was setting down her foot and Pa was offering the pup one more chance.

The pup continued growing and was soon a full-grown collie with long hair, white around her neck and the rest of her a golden-brown back to her tail, which tended toward black. She had a long nose with a black tip and a white forehead, ears that stood up and drooped a little at the ends, and the most piercing, knowing eyes I'd ever known an animal to have. When you talked to her, she tipped her head to one side and looked right at you with those eyes, clearly seeming to understand every word you said.

Fanny followed Pa everywhere. When he was plowing with the team, she trotted along behind him to the field and lay on the end, in the shade, watching the horses work. When Pa went for the cows, she trotted along behind, and soon began to learn that one of her jobs was to round up the cows and point them toward the barn.

One evening Pa asked me to take Fanny and fetch the cows for the evening milking; he was doing something he wanted to finish.

I followed the cow path up the lane back of the barn, through the little grove of oak trees that often served as night pasture, to the field that lay beyond. Fanny trotted along behind me, wagging her long bushy tail. She was rapidly becoming a good cow dog, and it was clear she enjoyed going for the cows.

We found the cows in the far corner of the pasture, resting under a big oak tree and peacefully chewing their cuds. A couple of them looked up when they saw Fanny and me approaching on top of a nearby hill. It was clear that they weren't ready to come for the evening milking and were enjoying their afternoon rest.

As Fanny approached, she barked a couple of times and circled the resting herd. I didn't say a word to her; it was something she had learned how to do from Pa's teaching. Slowly the cows got up, stretched, relieved themselves, and began walking toward the barn, switching their tails to scare off the flies that were a constant annoyance this time of year. One after the other, in a straight line, the cows followed the lane toward the barn. Fanny and I walked behind, in the little cloud of dust that rose from the cattle's feet. Fanny barked occasionally to let the herd know she was still there.

Fanny and our herd of mostly Holstein cows—we had two Jerseys that Pa said were there to put a little more cream in the milk—had a most interesting relationship. Sometimes, when the cows were in the barnyard, she would go out among them. The cows would nuzzle her as she wagged her tail and walked from cow to cow. It was clear to me then that animals could clearly communicate with each other, even across species.

The cows also had great respect for Fanny. She needed only to bark a couple times and they began moving in the direction she desired. Occasionally a high-minded cow, usually one of the younger ones, would challenge Fanny and refuse to do what she wanted. Fanny would bark sharply a couple times. If the challenge continued, Fanny nipped the disobedient cow on the heels. This action generally solved the problem and clearly re-established who was in charge.

Soon Fanny was going for the cows by herself. Pa had only to say, "Fanny, go get the cows," and she would wag her tail and trot off down the lane. A few minutes later the herd would come trailing down the lane. Fanny walked behind, barking occasionally to remind the cows of her presence.

One day a cow dealer stopped at the farm and wanted to look at the herd. It was the middle of the afternoon, a couple of hours from milking time. Pa sent Fanny to go after them, not knowing if she would at this unusual time. Just as she had done so many times before, the cows came walking down the lane and into the barnyard, with Fanny, her tail wagging, walking proudly behind.

"How much you want for that dog?" the cow dealer asked.

"Not for sale," Pa said.

"I'll give you $50."

"You haven't got enough money to buy Fanny," Pa said, as he rested his foot on the bottom board of the barnyard fence.

"How much money would it take?" The cow dealer was insistent.

"Not for sale," Pa said firmly.

Once or twice a year somebody tried to buy

Fanny, but Pa's answer was always the same.

Not only had Fanny become an excellent cow dog, she also had learned how to hunt squirrels. In fall, my brothers and I often hunted squirrels after school, in the big oak woods back of the house. We'd grab up our .22 rifles and would often bring home two or three of the furry little animals that Ma fried with onions, making quite a delectable dish.

One of the challenges of hunting squirrels was that if the squirrel saw you first, you never got a chance to see it. The squirrel either scampered off to its nest or a hollow tree, or merely hid high up on a branch and on the opposite side from where you were looking. When this happened, Fanny became indispensable. She had better eyesight than we did, and usually spotted a hiding squirrel long before my brothers and I did, especially if leaves were still on the trees. Squirrels were more fearful of Fanny than of my brothers and me. When a squirrel spotted Fanny, it slipped around to the backside of the tree, and, of course, that is where we learned to stand for an easy shot and squirrel in the skillet.

The years passed and we came to take Fanny for

granted. She never failed with her cow-fetching duties, squirrel hunting, and a host of other jobs she had around the farm, ranging from keeping a chicken from wandering too close to the house to announcing the arrival of a strange car in the yard.

I didn't notice the changes as much as Pa did, but I could tell he was concerned about Fanny. No longer did she willingly trot out for the cows but went along with one of us, or sometimes didn't go at all. The spring had gone from her step and the spirit from her eyes. He face had turned gray and the luster was gone from her coat. Sometimes she had trouble getting up and even wobbled a little when she walked. Pa said she had lost most of her sight.

One Sunday morning in May, after we had finished the chores, Pa announced that it was time to put Fanny out of her misery. He asked if I wanted to come along with him, to help him bury his longtime friend. I said I would help.

Pa took the 12-gauge double-barreled shotgun down from the hooks in the woodshed and shoved a shell into each chamber.

"Come on, Fanny," he said. The old dog couldn't get up. Pa lifted her back legs and helped her gain some balance. She staggered along beside him, her tail wagging slowly. I walked behind the pair, carrying a shovel and not at all looking forward to what I was about to witness.

Pa stopped in a little clearing on top of a hill in the woods. A bright sun lit the little area that was covered with purple violets, a beautiful sight.

Pa leaned the shotgun against a tree. He kneeled down by his friend and took her head in his hands. She looked at him through cloudy eyes and whimpered a little. I don't know what he said to his dog, but he talked for some time, quietly, his voice little more than a whisper.

Finally, he got up, retrieved his shotgun, and walked back a few paces from Fanny. He lifted the double-barrel to his shoulder and aimed. I could see that he was having trouble keeping the shotgun steady, a problem he never had, for he was one of the best shots in the neighborhood.

I couldn't watch any longer. Fanny lay looking at her master, wondering what he was doing. Never once had he harmed her in any way. In all their years together, he had never hit her, never even raised a hand to her. Not since her puppy years had he even raised his voice to her.

I looked off through the woods, at the new leaves appearing on the oak trees after many months of winter and bare branches. I tried to think about warm weather and spring work and fishing. I tried to take my mind off the scene behind me, in the little violet-covered clearing in the woods.

"Kaboom!"

The shotgun's report echoed through the woods, louder than I had ever known a 12-gauge shotgun to sound.

I turned to see Pa once more leaning the shotgun against the tree.

Fanny lay in the violets, a pool of blood staining the purple blossoms under her head.

"Grab the shovel," Pa said. "And start digging a hole next to her."

In a few minutes I had dug a hole that was three feet or so deep in the soft soil.

"That ought to do it," Pa said. We rolled the dead dog into the hole, and I covered her with soil, making a little mound on top.

Pa found a downed limb and pushed it into the ground on one end of the grave.

"That's it," Pa said. He turned for one last look at the grave. He took a big red handkerchief out of his pocket and blew his nose.

We walked back toward the house, neither of us saying anything. I heard a meadowlark call from the field just beyond the woods.

Coon Hunting

Pa had no love for raccoons. Raccoons had a nasty habit of getting into our chicken house and sucking the insides out of eggs, and when they found the garden sweet corn, it was destroyed in a couple of nights. Pa liked nothing better than to shoot a raccoon, but he seldom had a chance because raccoons did all their dirty work at night.

When Uncle Ed pulled into our yard one cool October evening just after we'd finished milking, Pa knew what he wanted without even asking.

"Bet Ed wants to go coon huntin'," Pa said.

Uncle Ed was older than Pa by several years, always had a week's growth of gray whiskers, and walked with a gait that allowed him to cover miles with little effort. Pa once told me he figured Uncle Ed had some Indian in him, but I guessed he meant he had outdoor skills like an Indian.

Once out of his old rusty Ford car, Ed opened the back door and two coonhounds bounded into the yard. They were the skinniest, homeliest dogs I had ever seen. They were a kind of a brownish liver color with short hair and long ears that flopped around when they ran. They didn't even bark like regular dogs, but made a kind of yapping sound, like they had sore throats.

"Get down, you hounds," Ed yelled as he swatted the one that was jumping up on Pa. The hound had his front feet firmly planted on the front of Pa's overalls.

"This here's Blue," Uncle Ed said. I thought it was a strange name for a dog, but I didn't say anything. "Other one's Nell. Best coonhounds you'll find anywhere around. If there's a coon in the woods, this pair'll track 'em down and tree 'em ever time."

Pa didn't know much about coonhounds, but if they could do what Uncle Ed said they could, he was all for it. Pa was intent on lowering the raccoon population no matter what it took.

"Good night for coon huntin'," Uncle Ed said. "Cloudy, no wind, a little dew to hold the scent for the hounds."

Pa crawled in the front seat of the car and I crawled in the back, along with Blue and Nell. Once the Ford started down the road, the hounds settled down and it was a calm ride. In the front, Pa and Uncle Ed talked about other raccoon-hunting expeditions—the sizes of the raccoons they'd gotten and every detail of the hunt, including how long it took for the hounds to tree a coon.

We drove a couple of miles or so south of the home farm, to an area that was hilly and heavily wooded. Three little lakes, once connected, stretched out along a long valley. Uncle Ed parked the Ford alongside the dirt road and we all climbed out, the dogs included. From the trunk of the car, Uncle Ed retrieved a single shot .22 rifle with the longest flashlight I'd ever seen taped to the bottom of the barrel.

"This here's all we need once these dogs tree us a coon," Uncle Ed said, patting the rifle. "Flash the light on him, aim at his head, and you've got yourself a coon, and a few more eggs left in the hen house."

Uncle Ed knelt down and put his arms around the neck of each of the dogs and began talking to them in a quiet voice. As he talked, their tails wagged and they began to shake all over. They seemed to know what he was talking about and what he wanted them to do.

"Time to tree us a coon," Uncle Ed finally said in a louder voice. "Find us a big 'un."

He released the dogs and they trotted into the woods, their long noses sniffing the leaf-covered ground. Immediately, they disappeared into the night. The three of us sat down under a big old oak tree. Pa and Uncle Ed each lit up cigarettes, which provided the only light in this black night.

As we sat under the tree, listening to the woods and hearing nothing, I wondered what we would do if the dogs treed a raccoon and we had to find them. It was impossible to see anything.

We must have sat under the old oak for nearly a

half-hour, listening and talking softly. I began to wonder what was so exciting about hunting raccoons. Nothing happened. Nothing at all. The cold October night began to seep through my clothes, and I shivered. I stood up and rubbed my hands together.

"What's the matter, Jerold? Cold?" Pa asked.

"A little," I answered. I didn't want to say that I thought raccoon hunting was just about the most boring thing I had ever done. I usually enjoyed being in the woods, but at night when there wasn't a sliver of light and nary a sound? Besides being bored, I was cold. I wasn't lying about that.

"Hear that?" Uncle Ed asked.

"Hear what?" Pa answered.

"It's old Blue."

"I don't hear nothin'," Pa said. I strained to hear, but I didn't hear anything either, just the deafening quiet of the night.

"Well, listen," Ed said. "It's old Blue all right, and he's picked up a coon trail."

Faintly, I could hear the baying of the coon dog far off in the valley beyond the second lake. It was just the hint of a sound to my untrained ear, but it was definitely a hound baying.

"I hear 'em," Pa said as we all stood forcing our ears to pick up the direction of the call.

"Got himself a hot track," Uncle Ed said. "Oughten be long 'fore we got a coon in a tree."

The baying became more clear as the hound circled through the big woods and around the lakes. The sound echoed through the valley, a kind of mournful sound that sent shivers down my back.

"There's Nell," Uncle Ed said. "She's joined him on the trail."

Uncle Ed could tell the two hounds apart by the sound of their voices; he also knew how hot or cold the trail was by the nature of the baying.

"It'll be a while 'fore they tree 'im," Uncle Ed said. "Trail could be hotter."

We sat down under the tree once more and listened to the hounds as they ran along the ridges, down in the valleys and around the lakes. Their baying was the only sound in the woods. I wasn't cold anymore; the excitement of hearing the hounds and the promise of a treed coon got my blood moving. Now I was becoming impatient with the hounds that seemed to take forever to tree the egg-sucking, corn-spoiling thief.

Abruptly the cadence of the baying changed; what had been measured had become a more excited, tightly paced yapping.

"That's it. They got the coon treed. Let's go," Uncle Ed said.

He grabbed up his .22 with the long flashlight attached and headed into the woods, with Pa and me stumbling along behind. I hoped he would snap on the flashlight, but he didn't. Just as he could hear better than either of us, he could also see better in the dark.

We ran full speed along a steep side hill, blackberry canes tearing at my denim barn jacket. We ran alongside one of the lakes. I tripped over a fallen tree limb and landed in a heap. Quickly I got up and ran faster to catch up with Pa and Uncle Ed as they ran toward the sound of the hounds calling "treed."

"Hounds are just ahead," Uncle Ed said. "Slow down. Don't want to spook the coon."

We walked slowly now, Uncle Ed not making a sound as he slipped through the thick woods. Pa could walk nearly as quietly as Uncle Ed, but I was a distant third in quiet walking as I tripped over down branches and tangled my feet in underbrush.

We were soon upon the hounds that were leaping up the side of a huge old oak tree. They were yapping so loud that I couldn't hear what Uncle Ed was yelling at them. Uncle Ed snapped on the long-barreled flashlight and began playing the beam of light over the upper branches of the tree, systematically going from branch to branch. The hounds kept up their frantic yapping and leaping.

This was the moment I had been waiting for. I had never seen a raccoon treed by hounds.

"You look for the coon's eyes flashing back at you," Uncle Ed said. I'd remembered how we often caught the eyes of a raccoon in our car's headlights when we were coming home from town on Saturday night. I imagined this situation was similar.

"There! There!" Uncle Ed said excitedly. "That's him! Got his eyes." Carefully, Uncle Ed aimed the rifle at the eyes that were reflecting light. He seemed to take a long time to shoot, aiming and aiming. I could see the eyes, too, but nothing more.

"Damn it," Uncle Ed said as he took the rifle from his shoulder.

"What's wrong?" Pa asked.

"Damn dogs treed a barn cat. That's a barn cat up there, not a raccoon. See?" Uncle Ed flashed the light on the tree limb, and I saw a big yellow cat, its fur standing on end and its mouth open, teeth bared. The cat didn't seem any too happy with what had happened, but nothing replaced Uncle Ed's anger.

"You worthless hounds!" Uncle Ed shouted. "Run us through the woods for a half hour and then tree a damn barn cat." He took a swing at old Blue with the rifle but the hound jumped aside.

"Gotta get me some new coonhounds."

Neither Pa nor I said anything as we walked back through the woods to the Ford, the hounds trailing behind us out of reach of Uncle Ed's anger. I wanted to say something to Uncle Ed about his exceptional coonhounds that preferred barn cats over raccoons, but I didn't think this was the time.

Rutabagas

Pa liked rutabagas. Ma ate them, but never said she liked them. My brothers and I didn't like them, but we ate them. We ate rutabagas in soup and with sauerkraut, cooked with pork hocks or prepared alone. Pa believed that if everyone had an opportunity to eat enough good rutabagas, they would like them. Nobody ever got around to telling him that just wasn't so.

I don't think I knew another kid that liked rutabagas; rutabagas were certainly not in the same category as sweet corn or even carrots, peas, or garden lettuce. Ma grew a few rutabagas in the garden, but Pa was never pleased with them, said they weren't right.

"What beggies need"—he called them beggies—"is breaking ground, not this soil that's been worked every year." Breaking ground is soil never before plowed. But by the time I was a kid, little virgin land, except for rough, wooded areas, remained in our county.

Pa had his eye on a three-acre patch of ground on the north edge of our woodlot. Slowly, over the years, we had cut trees from this land until now there were great open areas between the rotting stumps and remaining trees. The cattle had been allowed to graze there, so no new trees were replacing those we'd removed.

One day, as we cut down one of the remaining trees in the area for firewood, Pa said, "This land will grow beggies. Yup, beggies would grow good here. All we gotta do is break this ground and work it up."

The next spring, we began removing the remaining trees and stumps, no small task with a Farmall-H tractor and a team of horses. Pa had borrowed a breaking plow from somewhere, a single-bottom plow with

a huge moldboard and a knifelike coulter that cut through roots like they were spaghetti. We hitched the plow to the Farmall, which I drove while Pa hung onto the plow handles. We lunged across the field, slicing through roots, smashing into hidden rocks, and turning over the beautiful virgin soil that had never before been plowed. It was a back-breaking, miserable job for Pa. But he did it with a smile, because he had in mind rutabagas, beautiful, blemish-free, purple and white rutabagas. Rutabagas by the bushel that we would sell in Wild Rose, in Almond, Plainfield, Waupaca, Wautoma, all the towns in the area. Rutabagas for people who had trouble finding them in the grocery stores. Rutabagas for folks who prized those grown on breaking ground, or least that's what Pa believed.

With the plowing completed, we hauled load upon load of stones from the new field.

"Lord, this is a stony bugger," Pa said, sounding somewhat surprised that this fine piece of ground had such a major fault.

Pa bought a sack of rutabaga seed from the hardware store in Wautoma. "Want enough beggie seed for about three acres," he said.

"What'd you say?" the fellow at the hardware store asked, not believing his ears.

"Enough beggie seed for about three acres."

"Three acres of rutabagas?"

"Got a patch of breakin' ground," Pa said. "Best place there is to grow beggies."

"Well, here you are," the hardware store clerk said. "But you've cleaned me out. This is all the rutabaga seed I've got. It was supposed to be enough for all my customers. Most of them only plant a row in the garden."

The only way Pa could figure out how to plant the rutabaga seeds was to sow them by hand. So one Saturday I went with him to the breaking ground and he walked back and forth across the new field, flinging the seeds from side to side in about a twelve-foot swath.

Using the spike-tooth drag pulled with the Farmall, I smoothed off the field and at the same time covered the seeds. That was all there was to rutabaga planting. Now we had to wait to see if they'd come up—it was out of our hands. Mother Nature had to take over. We needed a gentle rain and warm weather. Not a gully washer because that would send all the seeds tumbling into the hollows, leaving the hillsides devoid of rutabagas and much of anything else.

A couple of nights later, a gentle, drippy rain began, the kind that occasionally fell in late May. The new field was properly soaked but not drenched.

A week later, when Pa and I were walking the new ground, we saw the first little rutabaga plants beginning to push through the soft, sandy soil.

"Yup, they're gonna come up," Pa said. "We did it right. Planted the field just right. Rain couldn't have come better."

Seldom had I seen Pa happier. We'd watched many cornfields coming up in the spring, and oat fields and alfalfa fields and potato fields, but I don't recall ever seeing Pa quite so pleased with a new crop. "Jerold, if the weather is good to us, we're gonna have beggies, lots of beggies. And we're gonna make some money too, more than we make on green beans and cucumbers."

I didn't say it, but I was thinking there must have been a lot more people who liked rutabagas than I thought there were. Of course, Pa ought to know where to sell the crop, he'd been in the farming business for a long time.

Green beans and cucumbers were the other two cash crops we grew for immediate sale. Every year we grew about an acre of each crop.

The weather was perfect for rutabaga growing. Sunny but cool days and ample rainfall. About once a week, Pa and I walked through the rutabaga field, noting the crop's progress. He would occasionally pull one of the little plants to see how well the root was advancing.

"Couldn't be better," he said one day in August. "I don't think I've ever seen a better field of beggies."

Of course, I had never seen a field of rutabagas, three acres of the crop in one place. But it was a sight to behold, if you are taken by beautiful, healthy rutabaga plants with scarcely a weed in sight. The purplish-green leaves nearly covered the ground for the entire three acres, a sea of waving, moving rutabaga plants foretelling a plentiful harvest of this wonderful but scarce crop.

"One of the beauties of breaking ground is no

weeds," Pa said. "Weeds come later, in a year or so. But look at that, not a weed in sight. Just beggies."

And so it was. Rutabagas everywhere, from where the woodlot ended to the road, on the hilltops and hillsides, and in the valleys and draws. The plants looked to be all about the same size, too. With regular cultivated ground, the hilltops usually supported poorer crops, and lush crops grew in the valleys. But not so with this virgin ground, where the natural fertility was the same on the hilltops and in the valleys.

The rains continued all summer, through August and into September, gentle rains that watered thirsty plants but left fragile soil in place. The rutabaga field continued to prosper. Neighbors driving along the road would inquire of Pa what was growing in that little field by the edge of the woods.

"You growing rutabagas in that field?" Guy York inquired one day.

"Yup, got me a patch of beggies on breaking ground," Pa replied with a smile.

"Awful lot of rutabagas, ain't it?" York inquired.

"Oh, a few bushels, I expect. People can't buy breaking-ground beggies these days. Everybody knows they're the best."

"People around here gonna buy all those rutabagas?"

"Yup. Once they find out I got these special beggies, we won't have no trouble moving 'em."

"Never figured there was that much demand for rutabagas, no matter how they're grown. I can't stand to have them around. Wife fixes a mess of rutabagas and they stink up the whole house. Those things got a powerful smell," York said.

"Ah, you're too much of an Englishman. If you had a little more German in you or a little Polish, you'd go for a good beggie. Did you know that beggies have medicinal qualities?" Pa asked.

"Didn't know that," York said.

"They do. It's the sulfur that's in them. Does wonderful things for the body, cleans the blood, purifies it, a wonderful tonic."

"It's the smell I can't get past," York said.

Finally the day came when Pa said, "Well, Jerold, let's dig that patch of beggies, see what we got."

We each shouldered a six-tine barn fork and walked the path through the woods to the beggie patch, as the field came to be known. We forked out rutabagas just as we would fork out potatoes, except the rutabagas weren't in rows, they were everywhere. Finally, Pa and I decided to take a three-foot-wide strip and work our way across the field, coming back with another three-foot-wide strip.

It was a beautiful sight—firm, round, purple and yellowish-white roots popping out of the ground with each stroke of the fork. I had never seen anything, anywhere, like it. Rutabaga roots carpeted the ground. There were hundreds of them, thousands of them. Some were as large as muskmelons; others were as small as onions. A few were long and thin, some were fat and squatty. Each was without blemish, and each was unique but also like every other one. By supper time, rutabagas lay everywhere. Few people, I'm sure, have an opportunity to stand in a sea of rutabagas, with the beautiful roots extending in every direction from hilltop to valley, from wood's edge to the road. It was a wonderful, unusual feeling to walk through the harvested field and have to carefully pick each step for fear of stepping on a harvested root.

Before we left the field that late afternoon to return to the house, we turned and looked once more at the beautiful sight. Pa was grinning like I'd never seen him.

"Ain't that just about the prettiest thing you've ever seen?" Pa finally said. "Wonder how many bushels we got here?"

I'd gotten so I could estimate how many bushels of dug potatoes lay on the ground before I picked them up, but rutabagas were something else. "Got no idea," I replied.

"Well, tomorrow we'll find out," Pa said.

The next morning, as soon as we finished the barn chores, we hooked the Farmall to the hay wagon, tossed on fifty empty potato boxes, and headed for the rutabaga patch. All day, my brothers, Pa, and I filled potato boxes with rutabagas, loaded them on the wagon, and hauled them to the cellar under the house. Pa kept count, and by suppertime, when we'd dumped the last bushel of rutabagas onto what had become a huge pile in the cellar, he proudly proclaimed the answer we all wanted to hear.

"Three hundred and fifty-two bushels of the best dang rutabagas you'll find anywhere in the Midwest,

anywhere in the country as far as that goes," Pa said, waving his hands over the pile like it was some kind of deity.

Pa wasn't much for exaggeration, but this pile of blemish-free, breaking-ground rutabagas triggered a response my brothers and I had not seen before. We'd never seen him more proud of anything he'd done in his farming career. On that day, owning a top-producing milk cow didn't hold a candle to raising this fine crop of rutabagas.

My brother Murf was the first to ask what I had been wondering about ever since I knew the crop was going to be a big one.

"Pa, we surely can't eat all these rutabagas. Take us ten years to do it."

Pa laughed. "Yup, take a lot of eatin' all right. What we're gonna do, we're gonna sell these rutabagas, all but a couple of bushel of them that we'll eat. We're gonna sell them to all those folks who've been waiting for breaking-ground rutabagas. I figure that's a lot of people."

"How are we gonna do that?" I asked. Pa had never talked much about selling the crop, only about

growing it.

"Easy," Pa said. "We're gonna peddle them. Peddle them from house to house. Sell them one bushel at a time. No time at all and we'll be out of rutabagas and wishing we had grown more. Just wait and see."

The following Saturday, we took the back seat out of the old 1936 Plymouth and piled it full of rutabagas. Pa gave us a quick lesson in selling.

"Here's how you do it," he said. "You each take a good-sized beggie, one that is perfect in every way. You walk up to a house and you knock on the door. When someone comes to the door, you say, 'We've got breaking-ground rutabagas for sale. How many bushels would you like? We're selling them for $1.50 a bushel.'"

It sounded simple enough. We began by driving down one of Plainfield's back streets.

"Lot of retired farmers live here. Bet they can't wait to sink their teeth into some breaking-ground rutabagas," Pa said.

We followed Pa's selling instructions, and my brothers and I each picked out a perfect rutabaga and walked up the sidewalk to the door of a little one-story house. It was a beautiful autumn day; the leaves had turned to many shades of yellow, red, and brown.

A gray-haired woman answered the door.

"What cute kids! What can I do for you?"

"See this?" I nervously asked as I thrust a rutabaga out so she could see it better.

"Yes."

"We're selling these and they are perfect in every way because we grew them on breaking ground and Pa says people have been waiting to buy rutabagas like this because there just aren't any like them and how many would you like?" I was out of breath when I finished my sales spiel.

"That's quite a lingo you got there, young man." The woman was laughing.

"I've been practicing," I said. "How many would you like?"

"How can I say no? I'll take one."

My brothers and I turned and ran back to the car. "Sold a bushel, sold a bushel," I said. We lifted a heaping bushel of rutabagas from the car. My brothers carried one side and I the other.

We stopped at the bottom of the steps where the gray-haired woman was waiting. She had a quizzical look on her face.

"Where you going with all those rutabagas?" she asked.

"You said you wanted a bushel. Here it is," I answered with a smile.

"My goodness. My goodness. I wanted one rutabaga, not a whole bushel. My goodness. I've never seen so many rutabagas."

I thought, *you should see the pile of rutabagas we have in our cellar if you want to see rutabagas,* but I kept my smile in place.

"How much do you want for one rutabaga?" She picked out a medium-size one, not even the biggest one in the box.

"I don't know," I stammered. "But I'll find out." I ran back to the car and asked Pa what we should get for one rutabaga.

"One beggie. She only wants one. Thought she wanted a bushel."

"So did I," I said.

"Charge her a nickel."

And that's how the afternoon went. A nickel here, a nickel there. Once in a while a dime for two rutabagas. Even one sale of a quarter for five. Not one person—not one—bought an entire bushel, so our old Plymouth was still half-full of rutabagas when we returned home.

"Off day," Pa said. "Too many widow women. They've forgot how good beggies can be, especially breaking-ground beggies."

The next Saturday was an off day, too. So was the following week and the week after that. By the time the snow began to fall and the peddling season closed, we hadn't sold twenty bushels of rutabagas. But Pa was ever optimistic. "We'll sell 'em in the spring," he said. "You know they make a wonderful spring tonic. Just what lots of folks need after a long winter."

In late March, I noticed a strange smell when I came in the house one day. I figured maybe that something in the pantry had spoiled. Ma was usually right on to such things, so I figured she'd take care of it. I didn't say anything.

A few days later, my Uncle Wilbur stopped by. He no more than got into the house when he said, "There's something dead in here. Something rotten." That did it. We all went looking for a dead rat or a woodchuck or some other critter that might have crawled into some odd corner of the house and died.

But nothing had died. The huge pile of rutabagas had begun to rot and they sent out a stench like one nobody had ever smelled before. It was stronger than chicken manure. Stronger than pig manure. Stronger even than a rotten egg. But here the comparison was close because the sulfur in the rutabagas formed a gas that smelled near like rotten eggs. So said Uncle Wilbur who seemed to know about these matters.

The following Saturday we hauled basket after basket of rotten rutabagas up the cellar steps and dumped them into the manure spreader. Pa hauled load after load of rotten rutabagas back to the rutabaga patch where he spread them.

"It's only fitting that they go back where they came from," Pa said. That spring we planted the breaking ground to oats and a finer crop of oats we'd never seen.

"At least the oats seem to like the rutabagas," Pa said.

Cutting Wood

Cutting wood wasn't the worst job on the farm, but it came close, especially if the temperature hung around zero and the snow was knee-deep or better. Woodcutting equipment consisted of a couple of double-bitted axes, which meant each had two cutting edges, and a two-man crosscut saw.

On a November Saturday that was snow-free with the temperature in the twenties, Pa and I shouldered our axes, grabbed up the saw and headed to the north side of the twenty-acre patch of woods that began just north of the house. When we were squirrel hunting earlier in the fall, Pa had spotted some dead oaks on the west side of the woods, and it was in this direction that we headed.

"Oak's the best firewood," Pa said. "Nothin' like oak for holdin' heat, whether you're bakin' bread in the kitchen stove or tryin' to keep the rest of the house from freezin'."

The smell of woods in fall is pungent and rich, a special kind of smell that is duplicated nowhere else. I breathed deeply as we walked quietly through the fallen leaves and around the blackberry bushes that were now naked of leaves but still had barbs that tore at your clothing and ripped your skin if you happened to walk into one. We didn't talk much while we walked. Pa always said, "Don't see nothin' if you're talkin'."

In the woods about twenty rods or so, I spotted a gray squirrel leaping from the branches of one tall oak to another, until it disappeared in a large leafy nest it had built high up in a big white oak tree. A few feet farther, a partridge flew up. As often as I had come upon a partridge, I still jumped when one exploded in front of me. The partridge's strategy saves its life—startle

your enemy so you have time to escape.

High up in another oak tree, on top of a hill, sat a lone black crow, looking down at everything around, a ruler of the forest. In winter, when the songbirds fly off to warmer climes, the forest is for the partridges, crows, blue jays, nuthatches and chickadees. While the blue jay announces your arrival into the woods with its "Thief, thief" call, the crow from its lofty perch lets you know that it is in charge, no matter what the jays say.

Soon we came to the trees that we had earlier seen.

"This looks like a good one," Pa said, as he rapped on an immense oak tree standing straight and tall in front of him. The tree was a good three feet across at the base. He walked around the tree a couple of times, looking upward all the while.

"Which way should we drop it?" he asked. He always asked me this question when we felled trees. Many factors had to be considered. Was the tree leaning? Were there other trees so close that the falling tree might get caught in their branches? From what direction was the wind blowing? Sometimes the way to fell the tree was obvious because the tree leaned toward an open area. But usually the decision was a complicated one.

"How about this way?" I answered, pointing toward the west.

"Ya-a-a," Pa said, allowing the word to drag out, inferring lack of agreement with me. "You see that little lean to the east? Make dropping it to the west kinda tough. But it probably could be done.

"I think we'll try this direction." He pointed toward the south, where there was an ample opening in the woods for the tree to fall into without tangling with a neighboring tree.

Pa took his double-bit ax, touched the blade against the side of the tree to show where he wanted to hit it, brought the ax back, and swung it forward with one mighty swing. "Thwack!" The blade cut deeply into the dead tree. He wiggled the handle a couple of times, removed the ax blade from the tree, and repeated the process. "Thwack!"

Soon wood chips flew as he continued notching the tree on the side where he wanted it to fall.

"That oughta do it," Pa said after a few minutes of

chopping. The notch was about six inches deep and a few more inches high. Pa grabbed up the crosscut and made a couple of tentative swipes across the trunk of the oak opposite the notch. Soon he had established the groove in which we would work.

"Grab hold the end of the saw and we'll see what this tree is made of." What he meant was we'd see whether the tree was hollow. I took one of the crosscut's handles and began pulling the saw, trying to remember Pa's words to never push and to allow the saw to do the work. I wondered, if the saw was doing all the work, why was I working so hard?

Pa pulled. I pulled. Pa pulled. I pulled. Soon a little pile of sawdust accumulated at my feet. Fresh sawdust has a slightly sweet smell that is not duplicated anywhere in nature. Smelling fresh sawdust is one of the fringe benefits of wood sawing, if there are any benefits from this arduous job.

Pa pulled. I pulled. Pa pulled. I pulled. Again and again. My arms began to ache, but I knew I shouldn't complain. Pull. Pull. Pull. The pile of sawdust came up to the first buckle on my five-buckle rubber boots. I felt the sweat beginning to ooze from my forehead.

"Time for a breather," Pa said as he let go of the saw. I stood up, stretched my back and allowed the feeling to return to my arms. They felt like the deadwood we were cutting, hanging off my shoulders like dry, lifeless tree limbs.

Then it was back to the saw. Remember only to pull. Don't push on the handle. Let the saw do the work. This advice echoed in my head as I tried to keep up with Pa, pulling as fast as he did, but not any faster and surely not any slower. Sawyers develop a rhythm, a way of sawing where the two of them become one. At times, I felt I was getting it, beginning to feel the oneness with Pa, but then it slipped away and I was a lone sawyer at the end of a saw with a stranger on the other end. One who was stronger and more experienced. One who knew when it wasn't working well for me but who didn't say anything because sawing wood, like so many things on the farm, takes experience, takes time. Takes patience and a willingness to learn. Takes being relaxed and not fighting the job. I was still fighting the saw, most of the time anyway. How could you relax when the saw was ever demanding? Pull. Pull. No time to slack off. No time to relax. Just keep pulling. Pull until your arms turn to putty. Pull until your arms fall off on the ground. Don't ever push, even when you want to push. If you push the saw it will pinch and stick. And then it won't go in any direction.

Now! Something different! The saw moved more easily and the groove grew larger. I heard a crack. A quiet crack, like a piece of kindling wood breaking. A few seconds later, a louder crack, a riflelike shot that echoed through the woods. The tree was beginning to tip and Pa was yelling "Pull out the saw! Pull out the saw!" And then he was yelling "Timber!" The huge oak was falling, crashing through the limbs of the trees around it, snapping at its base. With a huge "Whoosh!" and much cracking the tree landed right where Pa said it would. A few dislodged dead leaves filtered downward. Then it was quiet again, extremely quiet, after the thunderous explosion of the huge oak falling.

"Enough wood here for a week or two," Pa said as he grabbed up his ax and began chopping off the smaller branches. As he cut, I dragged the branches off to the side, stacking them into what soon became a huge brush pile.

"Rabbit house." What he meant was that rabbits always looked for a place to hide from predators, and brush piles were excellent hiding places.

Soon he had chopped off all the branches he could with his ax, and we grabbed the crosscut to slice the larger pieces, the ones that we would tote to the house. We cut the larger limbs into pieces twelve or fourteen feet long. The thinner the branch, the longer the piece. When we sawed the trunk of the oak, the pieces were only eight feet long.

And on to the second tree, and the third, and then it was time to walk home for dinner and rest a little, before returning in the afternoon to cut trees until it was time for evening chores.

By chore time, I was so tired I could hardly drag home. But Pa walked with a spring in his step, showing a kind of satisfaction that comes from a good day's work and the promise of firewood for our several stoves. For the kitchen stove and the one in the dining room, for the stove in the pump house that kept the pump from freezing, and the stove in the potato cellar that kept the frost off our crop of stored potatoes, and, finally, for the little stove in the stock tank that kept the ice away so the cows could drink.

Pa cut wood for several more days. School days, Weston Coombes, a neighbor, helped out.

"That Weston's a good man with an ax," Pa said. "Knows how to handle the crosscut, too." Weston thought woodcutting was about the best job there was, not like my opinion.

With the cutting finished, Pa and Weston hauled the trees to the house with a bobsled pulled by Frank and Charlie, since it had snowed several inches from the time when we cut the first trees. A long pile of wood, fifty feet or so and as tall as a man could reach, appeared near the house. The big pieces—eight feet long, some longer—were on the bottom; the spindly pieces, many twelve or more feet long, were on the top.

"Think we'll saw wood next Saturday," Pa said at breakfast one day shortly after the last trees had been hauled from the woods. Ma was on the phone shortly after breakfast, asking the neighbors if they could come over to help. Not too different from threshing, silo filling, or corn shredding, wood sawing was a community activity where all the neighbors helped. You, of course, helped them saw wood, too. Ma asked Frank Kolka and Guy York, Freddy Rapp and Alan Davies, Bill Miller and Arlin Handrich—the neighbors living closest to our farm. You didn't need as many people for wood sawing. But it wasn't the most pleasant job, especially if it was cold and snowy. Guy York owned the saw rig, which consisted of a wooden frame supporting a 36-inch circle saw on one end of a shaft and a drive pulley on the other. He powered the saw with an old Chevrolet engine he had bolted on the back of his ancient Ford truck. A drive belt was placed over the engine's pulley and the saw rig's pulley. York pounded a couple of iron stakes into the ground to hold the saw rig in place and the crew was ready to saw wood.

About all there was to sawing wood was carrying the wood up to the saw rig, placing it on a hinged carrier, and waiting for York to push the carrier with the wood toward the saw blade, which screamed its way through the piece. Nothing was quite as loud as a circle saw slicing through oak wood, not the sound of a silo filler, a threshing machine, or a corn shredder. It

was without question, the loudest piece of equipment to come onto the farm during the year.

While three or four men held the tree limb up to the saw rig, another grabbed the cut piece, now stove-wood size, and tossed it into a pile.

There were only two reasons for stopping—to move the saw rig because the pile of cut pieces had gotten so big it was falling back on the rig, or for the noon meal. By noontime, the crew had moved the saw rig three times. In the language of wood sawyers, they had sawed three sets of wood.

Ma was ready when the hungry crew filed into the house for a meal of boiled potatoes, fried ham, canned peas and corn, homemade bread, apple pie, and as much coffee as a man could drink. With the noon meal finished, York immediately cranked up the old Chevrolet engine, and wood sawing continued. There was no dawdling because everyone knew that by four o'clock it was already getting dark, and wood sawing was far too dangerous in poor light. It was dangerous enough when the sun was shining as the huge, screaming circle saw had no shield around it, but spun in the open. One slip and the saw would cut off a fin-

ger or an arm as easily as it sliced through oak wood.

By nightfall, six sets of stove wood stood back of the house, waiting for the splitting maul. The long pile of uncut wood had disappeared. The wood-sawing crew, a wet, tired group of men who had handled thousands of pounds of wood during the day, most of it wet and slippery, crawled into their cars and drove home for evening chores.

"This ought to hold us till March," Pa said. In late February we'd go back to the woods and do the job all over again.

Polio

Early in February 1946, on a day when the barn eaves were dripping and the path to the pump house was mushy, I came home from school with a sore throat. Ma said I was probably coming down with a cold.

"When you get in from the barn, we'll put you in bed and you'll feel better tomorrow," she said.

When I finished milking and doing the other barn chores, I felt awful. No cold had ever felt like this.

"I'll fix you a whiskey sling," Ma said. "And before you know it you'll feel better." A whiskey sling consisted of a couple tablespoons of whiskey in a cup of piping hot water. It smelled awful and tasted worse. This was Ma's standard treatment for a cold—and usually it worked. Once in bed, after consuming a whiskey sling, you broke out in a fierce sweat. Of

course, that was the purpose. According to Ma and her self-help doctor book, sweating meant purifying.

I was scarcely under the covers before I began to sweat, but the sore throat didn't go away; if anything it was worse in the morning.

"Guess you better stay home from school today," Ma said. "And stay out of the barn, too."

She stuck a fever thermometer in my mouth and, after leaving it there a few minutes, pulled it out and read the number. She held her hand to my forehead and said quietly, "You're burning up." She didn't have to tell me what I already knew. I crawled on the couch in the dining room and tried to sleep, but I couldn't. All I wanted was water. No more whiskey slings.

The next day I felt even worse. Except now something new had happened. My right leg began feeling numb, strangely numb, not like it does when it goes

159

to sleep and is all tingly when the blood rushes back, but just numb. I'd never had any part of me feel this way before, so there was no comparison I could make. The numbness went away after a day or so, and my knee began to hurt more than I remember anything hurting. Then slowly it began stiffening. I tried moving it often, and as I did it hurt even worse.

When Pa came in from chores the second night after I'd gotten sick, he said, "Move your knee," in a voice that meant I had better move it. But I couldn't, and tears came to my eyes when I said I couldn't do it.

"It hurts too much, Pa," I said.

The look in Ma's eyes said more than her words. I could see that she was worried.

"Herman, we've got to get this boy to the doctor. There's something wrong with him I've never seen before."

Ma and Pa were not much for doctors. They were accustomed to treating almost any illness that came along, whether one of their boys had contacted it or it was one of the farm animals that had taken sick. What was happening to me was clearly more than they understood.

They wrapped me in a quilt my grandmother had made and carried me to the Plymouth because my knee was bent and stiff and hurt so I couldn't step on my right leg.

At the doctor's office, Pa sat me down in the waiting room and Ma told the receptionist they'd like to see Dr. Hadden.

"You have an appointment?"

Ma answered that she didn't but hoped that Dr. Hadden could see me anyway.

"Well, you know you're supposed to have an appointment to see a doctor."

Ma said she didn't know that but would be sure to get an appointment if she was to come another time. She hoped that this time the doctor could look at her son without an appointment.

"Well, the doctor's awful busy and you'll have to wait."

"You want to look at a magazine?" Pa asked.

"My leg hurts too much," I answered.

It seemed like we had been waiting for hours (likely only a few minutes) when Dr. Hadden, a heavyset man wearing a white coat, came into the

reception room.

"What have we got here?" he asked in a pleasant voice—a considerable contrast to the receptionist, who busied herself behind the counter.

Dr. Hadden motioned for all three of us to come into a little back room, a shiny white room with a kind of bed in it. Pa half-carried me while I hopped on my good left leg.

Dr. Hadden instructed me to drop my trousers so he could look at my leg once Pa explained why we were there. I didn't remember ever dropping my pants in a strange place, but my leg hurt so much I didn't think much about it. I do remember that Ma had made sure I wore clean underwear before they loaded me into the car.

Doc Hadden ran his hand over my knee, squeezing a little here and there.

"Straighten out your leg, son," he instructed.

I tried to do as he asked, but I couldn't. The leg wouldn't work, wouldn't straighten out at all. As I tried, it hurt so bad I started to cry.

"How long has this been going on?" Dr. Hadden asked.

"Couple of days," Ma said. "We thought it was a cold or the flu. He complained about a sore throat and he had quite a fever."

"Not a cold," Dr. Hadden said. "Not a cold or the flu. Looks to me like it's one of a couple of things. It could be a kind of youth rheumatism or it could be ..." he hesitated a bit. "It could be infantile paralysis. Some call it polio."

"Oh, no," Ma said, bringing her hand to her mouth.

"It's still too early to think about infantile paralysis," Dr. Hadden said. "You watch him close for the next week or so. Check to see if he's able to move his leg. Give him lots of liquids and keep him warm. Come back in a week, and then we'll know better."

On the way home, Pa said something about me having rheumatism all right, and in a few days it would be better. He laughed and recalled how Gusty Miller (her real name was Augusta) had been complaining about her rheumatism this winter, more than she had in the past.

"Can you imagine," he said. "You and Gusty Miller havin' the same thing?" I laughed, too, the first time since I'd gotten sick.

A week later we were back to Dr. Hadden's office. My fever had mostly disappeared, and the pain in my leg wasn't as severe as it had been at first, but it still pained most of the time. Now my knee was absolutely stiff, frozen with a bend in it so that when I stood up the bottom of my foot stuck up in back. I couldn't walk at all and fell on my face when I tried.

Dr. Hadden examined my knee, asked me to move it, and inquired about how much pain I was having. I told him, as truthfully as I could. I believed I could stand a lot of pain. I'd been bumped, hit, and kicked by cows and stepped on by horses, but this was the worst pain I'd ever had. That's what I said.

"I've got to be honest with you," Dr. Hadden said as he looked at Pa and Ma. "I'm afraid this is infantile paralysis. This is the third case I've seen this month. Doesn't look good."

"What's it mean for Jerold here?" Pa asked. He looked right at the doctor, and he expected a straight answer.

"I'll be as truthful as I can," he said. "Looks to me like the disease isn't spreading. It's stopped right here

in his knee."

"But what about the knee?" Pa asked.

"He'll never walk again without crutches. I'm afraid he'll drag his bent leg the rest of his life," Dr. Hadden said. Ma looked down in her lap. I could see her eyes turning red.

"I think the paralysis has about run its course, and he ought to be feeling better in a couple weeks. The pain will slowly disappear," Dr. Hadden said.

On the way back to the farm, I sat in the back seat of the Plymouth, staring out the window at the white countryside, at the snow-covered hills and the woods. The enormity of what I had just heard began to wash over me. I would spend the rest of my life with a bent leg. This was the end of softball and deer hunting and traplines and skiing. It was the end of squirrel hunting and just walking in the woods in summer looking for blackberries, or not looking for much of anything, just enjoying the warm weather and the coolness under the oaks.

I thought of Junior Hansel, a young man whom I often saw sitting on his parent's porch as we drove by on County Highway A in the summer. He strummed on a guitar that had no strings, and he moved by crawling in the grass. He had something wrong with him; I never knew just what it was. People felt sorry for him, but mostly they ignored him, looked past him when they saw him, like he wasn't even there.

I began sobbing. My shoulders shook and I tried not to let Ma and Pa see my tears. But they heard, and Ma reached over the front seat and patted me on the leg. She didn't say a word. She didn't have to. I think she understood the agony I was feeling.

As Dr. Hadden predicted, the pain slowly disappeared as the days passed. Mother made up a bed for me in the dining room, so I was close by when I needed something. Miss Thompson, our teacher at Chain O' Lake School, began bringing schoolwork home for me. I looked at it in a halfhearted way. Nothing seemed important anymore. All I could think about was my paralyzed knee and how I would be unable to do my fair share of work on the farm.

By the first of April, after another visit to the doctor, I learned that the disease had run its course. Doctor Hadden said that except for my knee, I was just fine. I didn't know how he could say I was fine when my right knee wouldn't bend. I overheard him telling the folks about kids who had died from infantile paralysis during the past several months and how lucky I was to have only a stiff knee.

I walked by hopping on my left leg, with someone holding me up. Around the house, I moved by pushing a chair ahead of me. Pa had gotten me a wooden cane and I learned to walk with that, ever so slowly, by dragging my right leg and bracing myself with the cane. I fell down a lot, particularly when I tried to walk on rough ground.

On a sunny day in early April I walked to the barn, the farthest I had ever gotten from the house by myself. It took twenty minutes to get there. Before I got sick I could run to the barn in thirty seconds, maybe less when I was late for morning milking. I moved my left foot, firmly placed the cane, dragged my right leg forward, moved my left foot, and repeated the process. It was slow going and miserable. Each day I felt a little more sorry for myself.

One day in mid-April Pa took me by the shoulders and said, "You keep feeling sorry for yourself and you're gonna drive us all crazy. You wanna sit around

and do nothing, or do you wanna see how much strength you can get back?"

He had never talked to me this harshly before, except when I had done something wrong and deserved some punishment. Why was he punishing me for something that was not my fault? It wasn't my idea to have a paralyzed knee.

I didn't say anything but just stood there, leaning on my cane and looking down at the ground. I had lost twenty pounds during my illness, so I must have been a pitiful sight. A skinny kid who did nothing but drag around the house, complain, and feel sorry for himself.

"We got lots of tractor driving to do," Pa said. "It's time to put the oats in, and we gotta plow the corn ground. You're gonna help."

Was this Pa's strange kind of humor coming forth? He knew I couldn't drive the tractor; I couldn't even crawl up on the seat. I scarcely had enough strength to push in the clutch pedal with my left foot. What would I use to push in the brake pedal? My right leg was useless.

"I can't drive the tractor," I said, almost crying. "I

can't do anything, you know that."

"Well, you're gonna try tomorrow," Pa said. He had firmness in his voice that I seldom heard. He was intent on having me do something that I knew I couldn't do.

I hobbled out to the tractor shed the next morning, dragging my right leg and using my cane. It took me nearly five minutes to get there.

Pa was waiting for me. He had just finished gassing up the tractor.

"We'll tuck your cane in right here," Pa said, as he pushed it alongside the fender. Then he hoisted me up onto the seat next to him, and we drove to the oat field. I dreaded the thought of having to do something I couldn't do. What if the tractor got away from me, ran off like a frisky team of spooked horses that couldn't be stopped? What if I tipped over, smashed the tractor, and killed myself? What would Pa think then? I bet he would have second thoughts about asking me to drive a tractor again.

Once in the oat field, Pa hitched the tractor to the disk and said, "It's all yours."

I looked at him to see if he really meant what he

was saying, if he really knew what he was asking. All I saw was determination.

"Well, what're you waitin' for?" he said. "You forget how to run this thing?"

Of course, I hadn't forgotten. I had been driving tractor since I was eight years old. I knew how to operate it as well as he did. I just didn't think I could do it.

With all my might I pushed on the clutch pedal with my good left leg, and as I did, I eased the tractor into gear while pulling the gas lever enough so the tractor wouldn't kill when I let out the clutch. Slowly I eased out the clutch and the tractor and disk began moving forward. So far so good. But what was I to do when I had to stop? I knew I couldn't push in the brake pedal with my bad leg.

Pa stood at the end of the field watching as I slowly drove the tractor and disk across the rough plowed surface. The smell of fresh-turned soil mixed with the exhaust of the tractor. It was a good smell. A smell I remembered from the many other times I had disked with the tractor.

Soon I was nearing the end of the field and had to turn the tractor for the return trip. In preparation for the turn, I eased up on the throttle, but not enough, as it turned out. The front wheels began skidding in the sandy soil, and although the wheels were pointed for a right turn, the tractor continued moving forward. In situations like this, you stopped a skid and turned to the right by pressing the brake pedal for the right rear wheel—each rear wheel had its own brake. With my bad leg I tried to push on the brake pedal. I could scarcely touch the pedal to say nothing about pushing it. Had I remembered earlier to push in the clutch, all motion would have stopped. But I was so intent on making my bad leg work that I forgot to do this.

"Crack!" The sound of a wooden fence post breaking filled the air.

"Smack!" The front tires smashed into a stone and the engine killed. There was a deafening silence. The broken post with attached barbed wire leaned against the side of the tractor, still wiggling back and forth from the impact.

I crawled off the tractor to assess the damage, momentarily forgetting I couldn't walk. I fell into the freshly turned soil. At this moment the enormity of my disability engulfed me. I began pounding my fists into the dirt and sobbing, "I can't drive a tractor. I can't drive a tractor."

Pa ran the entire length of the field when he saw what had happened. When he got to me, in an out-of-breath voice he asked, "You all right?"

"I hate you, Pa!" I yelled. "I hate you! You made me do something I can't do! I hate you!" I was screaming as loudly as I could. Tears streamed down my face, and I was covered with dirt from the top of my cap to my shoes.

Pa brought back his hand as if to strike me. One thing my brothers and I learned well was we never talked back to Ma or Pa. If you did, you usually got a swift whack.

Before Pa's huge callused hand struck me he stopped. He allowed his hand to fall to his side. I saw a look in his face I had never seen before. It was a mixture of anger underlain by a look of profound sadness.

"Are you hurt?" he asked in a gentle voice.

"No," I said brusquely.

"Here. Let me help you up," Pa said as he slid his hands under my arms. "What happened?"

"Tractor got in a skid, and I couldn't push the brake pedal."

"Happens," Pa said. "I broke off a fence post once. Same thing happened to me."

"Bet you were able to push the brake pedal," I said.

"Didn't help. Tractor skidded into the fence anyway."

I knew what Pa was trying to do. He was trying to cheer me up enough so I would crawl back on the tractor and continue disking. I was ready to drag myself home, sit on the porch, and watch the cars go by. That's what a kid with a paralyzed leg was supposed to do.

With some stones, Pa propped up the broken fence post and twisted the wire tight with his pliers. "That oughta hold until we got time to fix it better."

Pa climbed on the tractor seat, backed up the machine, and pointed it in the direction it was supposed to go. I stood off to the side, holding onto a little tree in the fencerow for balance.

"Now, get back on the seat. There's lots of oat ground that needs disking," Pa said. He said it firmly. I wanted to say, No, I won't do it. But this would probably not be a good idea. I had already talked back to Pa once and gotten away with it. I was not so sure his patience, or sense of right and wrong, would allow a second time. He helped me on the seat, and I continued disking. Two or three times I tried to use my right leg for braking, but with no success.

But after a week of disking every day, I found I could push in the brake a little. And I could walk a little better, too. My knee was less bent.

The broken fence post was the beginning of my recovery.

Threshing

It was early August, dry and hot. The oat fields had turned from green to gold and it was time to start harvesting, backbreaking and grueling work, but also interesting and exciting. Pa and I pushed the grain binder out of the machine shed. It was covered with a year's accumulation of dust, dirt, and sparrow droppings. I swept the machine off with an old broom while Pa replaced broken sections in the sickle bar— the part of the binder that cuts the grain. We also stitched up holes in the canvases—heavy cotton cloth on which wooden slats were riveted. The canvases moved over wooden rollers and carried the cut grain from the sickle bar to the knotter, where a device strung a length of binder twine around the grain, forming a bundle.

It usually took two or three days to ready the old McCormick binder that had cut acres of oats. The bull wheel, a huge metal wheel with lugs that not only supported the binder but also provided the power to all the moving parts, was badly dented from dashing into and running over stones. Many of the metal guards that protected the sickle were twisted and bent, and at one time or another nearly every bolt had come lose from the constant collisions with rocks. But the machine still cut grain; that was the important thing.

On a hot, cloudless day, Pa hitched Frank and Charlie to the binder and drove out to the twenty-acre oat field that stretched from the road in front of the house to our farm's boundary with Griff Davies. Soon rows of oat bundles accumulated across the field as the team and binder slowly worked along, slicing off the standing grain and tying it into bundles that dropped to the ground. The binder was an interesting machine to watch. What you first saw was a reel, a series of wooden paddles that looked something like a big windmill, which turned and gently pushed the standing grain against the sickle bar. Once severed, the grain was captured by the moving canvas and moved to a second canvas that rushed it to the binding mechanism. The reel moved in one direction, the sickle in another, and the canvases in a third. With all of these opposing motions taking place, the entire machine moved forward around the field cutting five feet of oats at a pass.

I wasn't supposed to watch the binder; my job was to shock grain, to stand the oat bundles on their butt ends, ten or twelve bundles to the shock. Shocking grain wasn't the most pleasant job. You worked with your shirtsleeves down, as the cut grain was prickly and irritating to bare skin. To make a shock, you grabbed an oat bundle under each arm, and then stood up the pair with the head end of the bundles touching and the butt ends a few feet apart. One way to place the bundles just the right distance apart was to bend your right knee and stand the bundles over your knee.

You tried to make each shock as sturdy as possible so the wind wouldn't blow it over. Sometimes, if you didn't do it right, the shock fell over by itself. Like every other farm job, a certain pride went with shocking grain. You didn't want a neighbor to drive by and see half the oat shocks down, especially if there hadn't been any wind.

Slowly I made my way around the field as Pa continued cutting. The task seemed never-ending, especially when I looked at the few shocks I had made and then at oat bundles as far as I could see stretching across the field. When Pa finished cutting the field, he drove the horses home and joined me shocking the bundles. He was a much faster grain shocker than I was, and within a few hours the entire twenty-acre field of oats had gone from standing grain to row upon row of grain shocks. When we were finished, Pa took off his straw hat, fished out a red handkerchief, and swiped it across his forehead.

I had seen about all the grain shocks I wanted to see. I wondered what beauty city people saw in a field of grain shocks. Sometimes I'd see a car with an out-of-state license plate stop alongside an oat field, and somebody would take a picture. Whatever for? I wondered. For me a field of shocked grain represented a lot of sweat, scratched arms, and boredom. After the first hundred or so grain shocks, they all seemed alike.

"Isn't that about the prettiest thing you could ever look at?" Pa said as he looked across the field at our work.

I didn't say anything because he sounded just like the city people who "oohed," and "aahed" at the sight. At times like these I wondered about Pa. He seemed to see beauty in the darnedest places.

The rain held off and so did the wind. The grain shocks stood straight and tall, almost all of them anyway. A couple of mine collapsed, but Pa didn't say anything. He probably remembered that a few of the grain shocks he made as a kid toppled, too.

A couple weeks later, Bill Miller came over one night, after the milking was done. Pa, Ma, my two brothers, and I were sitting on the back porch enjoying the cool early evening and listening to the cicadas sing their raspy tunes from the top of the elm tree.

"About time to thresh," Bill said.

Bill and Pa owned a threshing machine together.

Besides threshing each other's grain, they also threshed the neighbors' grain crops. By now, all of the farmers in the neighborhood had finished cutting and shocking their grain, and they were waiting for the first one to thresh. You didn't want to thresh too early, before the grain shocks had sufficient time to dry, and you didn't want to wait too long either, because sure as anything it would start raining and then threshing would have to be put off until the shocks dried out again.

Nobody wanted to be first. People would think you were in a hurry. So everybody waited to see what Pa and Bill did.

"Yup," Pa answered. "About time. Grain's dried out pretty good. Wanna start at your place?"

"If that's all right with you, Herm," Bill said.

"All right by me," Pa answered.

The next day, Bill and Pa dragged the threshing machine out of the neighbor's shed where it was stored, and with Bill's tractor pulled it over to his place. It would take a day of greasing, tinkering, tightening, and adjusting before the machine would be ready for the threshing season. Bill was a better-than-average mechanic, so Pa took his lead in what to do. I came along to help where I could, which meant I scraped old grease and dirt off the machine, squirted oil in the oil slots, and mostly stood around in awe of the gigantic machine.

Without question, a threshing machine was the largest piece of equipment that ever came on the farm. The machine was three times as long as our '36 Plymouth, and three times as tall, too. It had belts and pulleys everywhere, some going in one direction and others the opposite way. Sticking out from the back end of the machine was a metal pipe a foot or so in diameter, which could be extended out twenty feet and with a hood on the end that could be adjusted with a skinny rope that led up to it. The pipe itself could also be moved back and forth with a handle. The oat stalks (now called straw) that remained once the grain kernels were removed blew out of the blower pipe onto the straw stack.

On the front end of the machine, sticking out over the tongue that was used to pull it, was a metal device a couple of feet wide and six or eight feet long and maybe five feet off the ground. This was called the elevator, and it was here that whoever was unloading grain bundles pitched them grain heads first. The elevator had a moving chain with crossbars that dragged the oat bundles into the craw of the machine.

The additional obvious feature of the machine, located about halfway back, was the grain chute. Once the grain was separated from its stalk, it was carried up to a little tank that held a half-bushel of grain. When the container was filled, it automatically dumped into a spout that had places to attach grain sacks at the end. There was room to attach two grain sacks, with a lever that allowed the grain to either flow to the left or right grain bag.

Besides these essential features of the machine, there were parts that shook, pulleys that turned, chains that moved over sprockets, a fan that blew out the straw, and an unseen part of the creature that groaned and growled when you fed the bundles too fast.

Before day's end, Bill backed his John Deere B tractor into the drive belt that ran from the tractor's drive pulley to the machine's pulley and slowly pushed in the clutch.

"Pop, pop, pop." The John Deere's two-cylinder engine labored as the threshing machine's many pulleys, belts, and chains began moving.

Bill eased the throttle forward a little, and the pops came closer together as the machine came up to speed. A cloud of dust began rising. Dirt, grime, and bird droppings that had accumulated over the many months of nonuse sifted loose. The threshing machine was like a big old horse shaking itself after a long rest.

Bill climbed down from the green tractor's seat and walked around the machine, looking and listening to make sure everything that was supposed to turn was turning, and everything that wasn't supposed to move didn't.

"Looks all right," Bill yelled to Pa over the noise of the machine.

"Don't like the sounds of the straw blower bearing," Pa yelled back. "Probably needs a little more grease."

He grabbed the grease gun, pushed it on the fitting, and pumped it a couple of times.

"Sounds better," Bill said, listening carefully.

"Looks like we can start threshing tomorrow," Pa said.

"Yup," Bill answered.

Right after supper, Mrs. Miller began calling neighbors to tell them they were gonna thresh tomorrow. Bill and Pa had figured out who should bring their teams and wagons, who should carry grain from the machine to the granary, who should tend the bagger, who should pitch bundles out in the field, and who should make the straw stack.

This year for the first time I was old enough to drive a team on a bundle wagon. Three other neighbors also drove wagons. The idea was to have enough wagons hauling bundles so the threshing machine never had to shut down.

When the dew was off—you never threshed wet grain, as it plugged up the machine and wet grain spoiled in the granary bin—I drove Frank and Charlie and our hay wagon over to Millers and out into their oat field, where Art Nordahl and Mac Jenks were waiting to pitch bundles onto my wagon. I drove the team from shock to shock and soon the bundles were piled on the wagon as high as a man could reach with a long-handled pitchfork. I moved the bundles around a little on the wagon, always having the butt ends toward the outside so the load wouldn't tip over or drop bundles when I drove from the field to the threshing machine.

When the wagon was loaded, I clucked to the team and we began the slow ride across the oat field to the country road that trailed past Miller's farm, and then into their farmyard and up to the side of the machine. Bill was idling the tractor, waiting for the first load of bundles—my load—to arrive.

I yelled "Whoa!" when the wagon was alongside the elevator and waited for Bill to push the throttle of the John Deere and bring the machine up to operating speed. Frank and Charlie fidgeted a little, as any animal might that had to stand so close to this enormous machine with all its belts and pulleys spinning and making a terrible racket.

"OK!" Bill yelled to me.

I began pitching bundles onto the elevator, one after the other, overlapping them ever so little, but not too much or the machine might plug.

Pitching bundles is like so many farm jobs where you do the same thing over and over. You try to develop a rhythm. With pitching bundles, you use your shoulders and your arms, as well as your legs. If you didn't learn how to use your whole body, you couldn't pitch off an entire load of bundles without stopping and resting. If you had to rest, you'd be the talk of the neighborhood.

About two-thirds through the load I could have surely used a rest. But I didn't slow up, couldn't slow up. Pa was standing by the machine, grease gun in one hand, listening to the machine work, and adding a little grease here and there. Out of the corner of his eye I knew he was watching me pitch bundles. If I didn't do it to his satisfaction he'd talk to me after the load was off, let me know how I could do things better.

Before I finished unloading, George Kolka pulled his load up on the other side of the machine. George was ready to begin pitching bundles when I finished.

With my load off, I drove the team under a shade tree and grabbed up the water jug that I knew was waiting there. I took a couple of long swigs on the jug before replacing the corn cob stopper and turning the team back toward the oat field for another load. One of the advantages of hauling bundles was you got a rest to and from the oat field. Some of the workers had no rest at all, like the field pitchers who went from one wagon to the next. But there were advantages to pitching bundles—it was quiet and clean in the field. Around the threshing machine, you couldn't talk without yelling and dust was everywhere.

A beginning job on the threshing crew was shoveling back oats in the granary. Kids as young as eight or nine had this job. It was tiring, monotonous, and never-ending. Just when you thought you'd caught up, another man would come through the granary door with a filled sack of grain and dump it right in front of you so you had to keep shoveling.

The elderly farmers in the neighborhood, those who couldn't pitch bundles, carry oat bags, or drive a bundle wagon anymore, tended the bagger. This meant filling each oat bag and replacing the filled bag with an empty one. It wasn't hard work, and the old guys seemed to enjoy having any kind of job around the threshing rig. Another old guy's job was tending the straw blower, moving it occasionally so to con-struct a decent-looking straw stack. Straw stacks sometimes got nearly as tall as the barn, especially if the farmer had thirty or more acres of grain and it was a good year. Oat straw was valuable—farmers used it for bedding livestock throughout the long winter.

One more threshing job must be mentioned. Some threshing machine operators—Pa and Bill were not exceptions—had you believe that the man on the straw stack with a long-tined fork had the best job of everyone threshing. It was the worst kind of lie, because trying to build a straw stack with a long-tined fork while the straw was blowing on top of you and your footing was always shifting came close to being the worst job on the farm. It was right up there with forking rotten potatoes out of the cellar and cleaning out the pig house on a hot day in July.

Somebody had to be on the stack and the only way to convince someone who didn't know better was to tell him how great was the job. About the only guy who'd work the stack was a kid who hadn't done it before, or somebody who knew the job had to be done and did it, no matter how miserable it was. Every community had a couple men who would do the miserable jobs. I wasn't one of them.

At noontime Bill shut down the machine and everyone filed into Miller's house, where Lorraine Miller and my mother had been working since early morning to prepare the noon meal. One of the truly grand features of threshing was eating monstrous threshing meals. The only meal that would come close to a thresher's dinner might be Thanksgiving, and sometimes Thanksgiving dinner would have to take second place. We sat down to platters of roast beef, bowls filled with mashed potatoes topped with hunks of butter, dishes of carrots and peas, dill pickles, thickly sliced homemade bread, and at least three kinds of pies, each cut into five pieces. Whole pies of apple, cherry, and lemon meringue were passed around, and you scooped out a piece or sometimes even two. The cooks kept the coffee cups filled and constantly replenished the empty platters and bowls. In a few short minutes, we all pushed back from the table and staggered outside to sit under the shade tree for a few minutes.

The conversation ranged from the older men talking about corn and milk prices to younger guys discussing who was taking out which girl. It was a time for storytelling and yarn spinning. It was a time for renewing connections with neighbors we hadn't seen much all summer because they were busy with their own farm work.

Right in the middle of a deer-hunting story that Arlin Handrich was spinning, Bill Miller, who was sitting off to the side, announced it was time to crank up the machine or we wouldn't get done this afternoon. We'd wait until supper to hear the rest of Arlin's story.

Load after load of oat bundles pulled up to the threshing machine all afternoon, and at five o'clock the last bundle was pitched onto the elevator. A few minutes later Bill shut down the machine and it shuddered to a stop. Once more the threshers filed into the house for supper, another extravaganza of good food.

Each year, as we moved from farm to farm, we knew some of the cooks were better than others. When there was an especially good cook, we might even slow the work some, with the hope of getting an additional meal. When we came to a farm with a poor cook, we speeded things up so we didn't have to eat more than one meal at the place.

After supper, I glanced at the enormous stack of golden yellow straw dwarfing the threshing machine that stood next to it. I stopped at the granary to have a look at the filled grain bins. The smell of freshly threshed oats, sprinkled with the sharp tang of ragweed seed, engulfed me as I stepped inside. Three oat bins were filled to the top—800 bushels of grain, the counter on the threshing machine said, enough oats for Bill's cows and chickens for the coming year and enough left to plant the fields the following spring.

After he finished with the evening chores, Bill pulled the threshing machine over to our farm and set it up for the next day's work. Threshing would go on day after day, weather permitting, until all the farmers' grain in the neighborhood was threshed, the oat bins were full, and the straw stacks piled high. In two weeks, threshing season would be another memory.

The Day the Cows Were Sold

A gray, heavy sky hung low as I drove to the farm that late March afternoon in 1964. Pa was planning to sell the milk cows; the auction was scheduled for the following day. Auctions, pleasurable events for those attending, are seldom pleasant for those who are selling. Especially when the sellers are farm people. An auction usually signals a major change—death, financial difficulty, or retirement.

Retirement was the reason for this farm auction: Pa's retirement from milking cows, something he had done twice a day, everyday, for nearly forty years. You could count on one hand the days he had missed a milking. Pa would reach sixty-five the next year, and he had decided to sell his small herd of registered Holstein cattle. None of his three sons had stayed on the farm but had moved to cities for work.

I arrived at the farm at supper time. An extra place had been set for me at the kitchen table, the same place at which I had sat during all my growing-up years. Pa's place was on one end of the table, my mother's on the other. For forty years, they had sat in the exact same place, likely not different from other farm couples who had established a routine and stuck to it. I hadn't paid much attention to my father's aging; in fact, I was taken aback when I first heard about the auction. He was still healthy, vigorous, and able to do the farm work that he so much loved, but he had been complaining about his knees a little more each year. "Milker's knee" was the problem, a rather common complaint among dairy farmers, who twice a day stooped under cows to fasten milking machines and, a few minutes later, remove them. A knee can only take so much bending, and forty years of bending, twice a day, eventually takes its toll.

Pa had been bald as long as I could remember. Now the hair around his ears and on the back of his head was a silver gray. This was the first time I had really noticed. As with other farmers who spent considerable time outdoors, the top of Pa's head was chalky white, the bottom part a fading tan that became a deeper tan as spring and summer work kicked in. He always wore a cap in winter and a straw hat in summer, which accounted for the color difference.

Ma's hair had turned gray as well, and she moved a little more slowly than I'd remembered. But her cooking hadn't changed. There was a bowl of steaming boiled potatoes, home-canned green beans, slabs of fried ham, and fresh-baked apple pie. All foods my mother knew I liked.

Talk around the table was about the auction the following day and whether all the details had been taken care of.

"Weatherman predicts snow for tonight," Ma said. Pa didn't say anything. He looked worried, but it was hard to know whether he was concerned about the weather or the fact that soon he'd have no cows to milk. I was sure it was the latter that bothered him, but he never would have said so.

That night it snowed several inches—wet, heavy snow typical for March. I got up at 5:30, as I had when I lived at home and was old enough to milk cows. I walked through the snow to the barn, memories of earlier days filling my head. Pa was already there, slipping the milking machine on the first Holstein in line. Since his sons had left home, he had developed a routine that worked well for him.

"You can feed the calves," he said as he poured milk into two calf pails. I did as I was told, remembering that I fed the calves when I was still too young to milk cows. Feeding calves introduced you to the work in the dairy barn.

Usually Pa was quite talkative as he moved from cow to cow, putting on the two milking machines, removing them, pouring the milk from the milking-machine buckets into a strainer on top of a ten-gallon milk can standing in back of the cows. But it was quiet in the barn this morning, the only sounds the pulsating "whoosh" of the milking machines and the cattle rattling the metal stanchions that confined them in their stalls.

Pa was some other place, it seemed. Or perhaps the other place was this place, when some of his best cows were calves and he wondered how they would turn out. Or when a top-producing cow died unexpectedly and not even the vet knew why. Or before milking machines, when we milked cows by hand.

I remembered that milking by hand was a wonderful time for thinking. It was warm and comfortable nuzzled up to the flank of a cow, especially one that enjoyed being milked. Now and again a cow didn't like having her teats pulled or perhaps just didn't like you, and seemed to enjoy trying to put her foot in the milk pail or kicking at you. These miserable, uncooperative beasts were exceptions, thankfully. The worst ones Pa milked himself, cussing at them each time he did. Finally, Pa gave up on most of the "kicker cows" and shipped them off to market, or sometimes sold them to a cattle dealer who didn't bother to ask if they kicked.

"No need to offer such information," Pa said. "Fellow that buys the cow will find out soon enough."

With milking finished and hunks of baled hay spread out in front of the cows, we toted the three cans of milk—thirty gallons total—to the milk house. One last time, Pa slipped the cans into the cooling tank and flipped on the water pump so that fresh water would flow around the cans.

"Arvilla called and said the roads are a little slippery," Ma said when we came into the house for breakfast. Arvilla was my mother's younger sister. She had planned to come out to the farm to help around the house during the auction.

"Hope the snow doesn't keep buyers away," Ma added.

Pa didn't reply, but I could see that he was concerned. The auction was scheduled to start at 10 a.m. Don Steege, the auction manager, arrived at 8.

"Roads will be OK as soon as the sun comes out," he said. "But we'd better get out there and shake the snow off the sale tent before it goes down." He motioned for me to help. The tent was white and blue striped, about forty feet long by twenty feet wide. The sales crew had erected it the previous day. The tent provided some shelter from the March winds, but no one had anticipated the late March snow.

The first buyers began arriving about 8:30. They walked through the barn, eyeing the cows and comparing each one to her written description. One of Steege's jobs had been to write a summary for each cow, including its milk production record, butterfat test results, and family background. Each cow had a pedigree, a written account of its parents—dams and sires they are called. Dams are the mothers, and sires are the fathers.

Promptly at 10, the auctioneer, Colonel Sonny Bartel of Hastings, Minnesota, took his place at the podium, grabbed up the mike, and welcomed everyone to the sale. One of the ringmen had led the first cow into the tent a few minutes earlier. It was one of Pa's best cows; not the best, but one of the top producers.

"It's part of auction psychology," Steege said. "Sets the pace for the rest of the auction. Price we get for the first animal is important."

Steege, a tall, thin, middle-aged fellow, read off the essentials on this first cow, including her official name, June Abbekerk Marathon, her rather outstanding pedigree, and her record of well-above-average milk production, with a butterfat average of 3.8 percent.

The cow, unaccustomed to being led and a little upset with the crowd staring at her, planted all four feet and just stood. A gentle slap on the rump by the second ringman got her moving again.

"Who's willing to start it off?" the auctioneer asked.

"What do I hear, who'll give me five hundred dollars, do I hear five hundred, who's got five hundred?" the auctioneer chanted.

"A hundred," said someone from the front row.

"Got a hundred, who'll give me two, who'll give me two bills for this fine Holstein cow? Can't go wrong with her. Look at her record. Don't see many records like this one. Who'll say two, two, two, do I hear two, who'll give me two?"

Slowly the bids went up until they reached $275. The auctioneer, sensing he'd gotten the cow up about as high as he could, said, "Are you through? Anymore? I'm gonna sell her. Once, twice, sold to number 165, sitting right here in the front row."

Cow after cow was led into the ring, interspersed with heifers and calves. Before the sale was over, twenty-seven cows, heifers, and calves went before the auctioneer and were gaveled off to buyers from throughout the region. The highest-priced cow sold for $710; the amount received for the entire herd was $8,608, making the average price per animal about $320. The auction company took twelve percent, leaving $7,575 for the herd.

By three o'clock that afternoon, the last cow had been led out of the ring, and trucks began taking turns backing up to the barn and loading cattle. Most of the animals had never seen the inside of a truck, so loading was a challenge. There was considerable cursing and rump slapping, but by five the last cow was loaded, and the truck slowly pulled out of the yard, cutting ruts in the driveway left soft by the wet snow.

An hour later, Don Steege handed Pa a check for the auction receipts, after sales fees, tent rental, advertising, and auctioneer expenses had been deducted. Pa stared at the check but said nothing. What can be said when most of your life's work is represented on one small piece of paper with some numbers and a signature scratched on it?

It was supper time, and the three of us again sat around the kitchen table. All the cars, trucks, and people had left.

"How'd it go, Herm?" Ma asked.

"Coulda been a lot worse," Pa replied. "Coulda been a lot better, too." He'd hoped the cows would have sold for more, but with an auction you always take your chances.

No other words were spoken as we ate fried potatoes, ring bologna, and homemade bread.

After supper, Pa and I walked to the barn, leaving the milking machines behind in the milk house. The barn was eerily quiet and cold without the animals to keep it warm. The single row of stanchions stood empty, as if waiting for the cows to come in for the evening milking. There was a faint smell of alfalfa hay and corn silage in the air, mixed with the more pungent smell of cow manure. Not unpleasant smells for a dairy farmer.

Pa stood behind the cow stalls. I stood nearby but neither of us said anything. When he turned toward me, I could see tears in his eyes. It was one of the few times I'd seen my father cry.

"Musta got some dust in my eye," Pa said as he pulled a red handkerchief out of the back pocket of his overalls and blew his nose.

Other Books by Jerry Apps
from Amherst Press

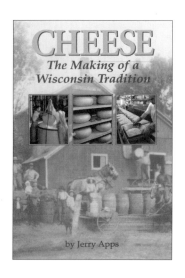

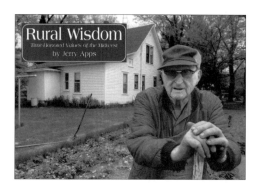

For more information about books by Jerry Apps,
or other regional interest titles and cookbooks, call

Amherst Press 1-800-333-8122

and ask for a FREE catalog.

You can also reach us by fax at 715-358-9456
or by email at Amherst@newnorth.net